Building TOEIC® L&R Test Skills

スキルアップ TOEIC® L&R テスト

Tyler Burden
Tsuyoshi Chiba
Yau-Sin Cheng
Kiyoshi Fukasawa
Akio Homma
Takamasa Fukuoka

NAN'UN-DO

Download Audio

音声ファイル
無料 DL
のご案内

このテキストの音声を無料で視聴（ストリーミング）・ダウンロードできます。自習用音声としてご活用ください。
以下のサイトにアクセスしてテキスト番号で検索してください。

https://nanun-do.com テキスト番号［**512071**］

※ 無線 LAN（WiFi）に接続してのご利用を推奨いたします。

※ 音声ダウンロードは Zip ファイルでの提供になります。
お使いの機器によっては別途ソフトウェア（アプリケーション）の導入が必要となります。

※ Building TOEIC L&R Test Skills 音声ダウンロードページは以下の QR コードからもご利用になれます。

本書の音声マーク につきまして

02 学習者への提供音声（添付 CD、音声ダウンロードサービスでの提供）

T-CD 1-02 教授者への提供音声（教授者用 CD での提供）

Building TOEIC® L&R Test Skills

by
Tyler Burden
Tsuyoshi Chiba
Yau-Sin Cheng
Kiyoshi Fukasawa
Akio Homma
Takamasa Fukuoka

TOEIC® Listening & Reading Test について

TOEIC® (Test of English for International Communication) とは、アメリカのテスト専門機関 ETS (Educational Testing Service) が開発及び製作した、国際的コミュニケーション能力を測定するテストの総称です。中でも TOEIC® Listening & Reading Test は、英語力を測定するテストとして、日本の多くの企業で採用や昇進などの際に活用されています。

1. テスト形式と特徴

リスニングとリーディングの能力を測定するマークシート方式の一斉客観テストで、以下の特徴があります。

- テストは全て英文。日本語は一切使われない。
- 英文和訳や和文英訳などの設問は出題されない。
- 日常及びビジネスのコミュニケーション場面を想定した問題設定。
- アメリカ・イギリスだけでなく、カナダ・オーストラリア・ニュージーランドの発音を採用。

2. 試験時間と問題数

リスニングの試験時間は約 45 分で出題数は 100 問、リーディングの試験時間は 75 分で出題数は 100 問、合計、出題数が 200 問の約 2 時間のテストです。

3. テストの結果

テスト結果は、990 点を満点とするスコアで評価されます。リスニングとリーディング、どちらもそれぞれ 5 ～ 495 点の範囲で 5 点刻みで評価します。

TOEIC® Listening & Reading Test 問題構成

	パート名		問題数
リスニングセクション　Listening Section（約 45 分間）			
Part 1	写真描写問題	Photographs	6
Part 2	応答問題	Question-Response	25
Part 3	会話問題	Conversations	39
Part 4	説明文問題	Talks	30
リーディングセクション　Reading Section（75 分間）			
Part 5	短文穴埋め問題	Incomplete Sentences	30
Part 6	長文穴埋め問題	Text Completion	16
Part 7	一つの文書	Single passages	29
	複数の文書	Multiple passages	25

教科書の構成

この教科書は、日常的な話題をテーマにしたリスニング問題のユニットと、文法事項を中心としたリーディング問題のユニットが交互に配置されています。どちらも TOEIC® Listening & Reading Test の問題に準拠した問題で、英語学習の初心者でも無理なく学ぶことができます。TOEIC® Listening & Reading Test の問題を学習しながら、英語を学ぶ上で必要な語彙や表現を身に付けることを目指しています。

◉リスニングの構成

Useful Tips ではリスニングの基本的な知識を学習します。Challenge ではリスニング学習に慣れるための語彙や基礎的な英会話表現を学習します。

Part 1 Photographs　写真描写問題

写真を見て、最も適切に写真を説明している文を選びます。

Part 2 Question-Response　応答問題

まず、最初の話者の質問、あるいは発言を聞きます。その後、2番目の話者による3つの応答を聞きます。最初の話者への応答として最も適切なものを選びます。

Part 3 Conversations　会話問題

会話を聞き、質問に対する最も適切な答えを選びます。

Part 4 Talks　説明文問題

アナウンスやナレーションなどのショート・トークを聞き、質問に対する最も適切な答えを選びます。

◉リーディングの構成

文法事項の説明

基本的な文法事項を取り上げて、例文を挙げて解説しています。
Exercise 1 では、問題を解きながら、取り上げた文法事項を再確認します。
Exercise 2 は、単語の意味を確認する問題です。取り上げた単語は、次ページ以降に出てくる単語が選択されています。問題を的確に理解する上で、重要な単語の意味を確認してください。

Part 5 Incomplete Sentences　短文穴埋め問題

短文が完成するよう、空所に入る最も適切な単語・語句を選びます。

Part 6 Text Completion　長文穴埋め問題

長文が完成するよう、空所に入る最も適切な単語・語句を選びます。

Part 7 Reading Comprehension

英文を読んで、設問に対する最も適切な答えを選びます。
Unit 2 と Unit 8、Unit 15 では、英語の文書は1つで、設問は3問です。
Unit 4 と Unit 10 では、英語の文書は2つで、設問は4問です。
Unit 6、Unit 12、Unit 14 では、英語の文書は3つで、設問は5問です。

Contents

TOEIC® Listening & Reading Test について
教科書の構成

Unit 1 Shopping (1) 〈Listening〉 7
Part 1 Photographs 写真描写問題
Part 2 Question-Response 応答問題
Part 3 Conversations 会話問題
Part 4 Talks 説明文問題

Unit 2 Shopping (2) 〈Reading〉 11
Part 5 Incomplete Sentences 短文穴埋め問題
Part 6 Text Completion 長文穴埋め問題
Part 7 Reading Comprehension 1つの文書

Unit 3 Food (1) 〈Listening〉 17
Part 1 Photographs 写真描写問題
Part 2 Question-Response 応答問題
Part 3 Conversations 会話問題
Part 4 Talks 説明文問題

Unit 4 Food (2) 〈Reading〉 21
Part 5 Incomplete Sentences 短文穴埋め問題
Part 6 Text Completion 長文穴埋め問題
Part 7 Reading Comprehension 2つの文書

Unit 5 Family (1) 〈Listening〉 28
Part 1 Photographs 写真描写問題
Part 2 Question-Response 応答問題
Part 3 Conversations 会話問題
Part 4 Talks 説明文問題

Unit 6 Family (2) 〈Reading〉 33
Part 5 Incomplete Sentences 短文穴埋め問題
Part 6 Text Completion 長文穴埋め問題
Part 7 Reading Comprehension 3つの文書

Unit 7 Music (1) 〈Listening〉 40
Part 1 Photographs 写真描写問題
Part 2 Question-Response 応答問題
Part 3 Conversations 会話問題
Part 4 Talks 説明文問題

Unit 8 Music (2) 〈Reading〉 44

Part 5 Incomplete Sentences 短文穴埋め問題
Part 6 Text Completion 長文穴埋め問題
Part 7 Reading Comprehension 1つの文書

Unit 9 Amusement (1) 〈Listening〉 50

Part 1 Photographs 写真描写問題
Part 2 Question-Response 応答問題
Part 3 Conversations 会話問題
Part 4 Talks 説明文問題

Unit 10 Amusement (2) 〈Reading〉 54

Part 5 Incomplete Sentences 短文穴埋め問題
Part 6 Text Completion 長文穴埋め問題
Part 7 Reading Comprehension 2つの文書

Unit 11 Pubs (1) 〈Listening〉 61

Part 1 Photographs 写真描写問題
Part 2 Question-Response 応答問題
Part 3 Conversations 会話問題
Part 4 Talks 説明文問題

Unit 12 Pubs (2) 〈Reading〉 66

Part 5 Incomplete Sentences 短文穴埋め問題
Part 6 Text Completion 長文穴埋め問題
Part 7 Reading Comprehension 3つの文書

Unit 13 Countryside (1) 〈Listening〉 74

Part 1 Photographs 写真描写問題
Part 2 Question-Response 応答問題
Part 3 Conversations 会話問題
Part 4 Talks 説明文問題

Unit 14 Countryside (2) 〈Reading〉 79

Part 5 Incomplete Sentences 短文穴埋め問題
Part 6 Text Completion 長文穴埋め問題
Part 7 Reading Comprehension 3つの文書

Unit 15 Mini-TOEIC® Test 〈Listening & Reading〉 87

Part 1 Photographs 写真描写問題
Part 2 Question-Response 応答問題
Part 3 Conversations 会話問題
Part 4 Talks 説明文問題
Part 5 Incomplete Sentences 短文穴埋め問題
Part 6 Text Completion 長文穴埋め問題
Part 7 Reading Comprehension 1つの文書

Unit 1 Shopping (1)

Useful Tips 発音・リスニング　トレーニング

「早口言葉」は英語で Tongue Twisters と言いますが、これは発音やリーディングの向上に効果的なツールです。次の文を声に出して読んでみましょう。

① **I scream, you scream, we all scream for ice cream.**
（私が叫ぶ、あなたが叫ぶ、アイクリームが食べたいとみんなが叫ぶ。）
scream for ～ で、「～を求めて（欲しくて）叫ぶ、声をあげる」 最後の ice cream が、最初の I scream と同じ音になっているので、何度も繰り返していると、何がなんだか分からなくなってきます。

② **She sells sea shells by the seashore.**
（彼女は海辺で貝を売っている。）
コツは、語頭の発音、/s/（sell、sea）と /ʃ/（She、shell、shore）の違いをはっきりさせることです。

③ **Fred fed Ted bread, and Ted fed Fred bread.**
（フレッドがテッドにパンを与え、テッドがフレッドにパンを与えた。）
すべての語が /d/ で終わりますが、語尾の /d/ の発音を抑え気味にして次の単語につなげるようにします。

Challenge

A. Match the words on the left to their definitions on the right.

1. merchandise	(a) a voucher that allows one to get a service
2. annual	(b) goods to be bought and sold
3. expiry	(c) the end of the period
4. coupon	(d) expensive
5. pricey	(e) occurring once every year

B. Choose the correct responses to each question / statement on the left from among the responses on the right.

1. I'd like to exchange this sweater, please.
2. Is this dress on sale?
3. Can you tell me where the produce section is?
4. What are you working on?
5. When do you want it delivered?

(a) It's in aisle D.
(b) Do you have the receipt?
(c) I'd like it delivered tomorrow.
(d) I'm figuring out my budget.
(e) I'm afraid the sale ended yesterday.

Part 1 Photographs

02 T-CD 1-02

For each picture, you will hear four short statements. Look at the pictures below and choose the statement that best describes what you see in each picture.

1.
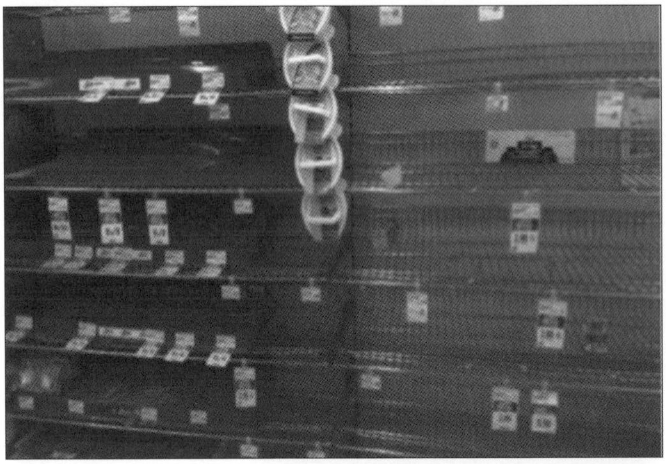
Ⓐ Ⓑ Ⓒ Ⓓ

2.

Ⓐ Ⓑ Ⓒ Ⓓ

Part 2 Question-Response

03 T-CD 1-03

Choose the best response to each question or statement you hear.

3. Mark your answer. (A) (B) (C)
4. Mark your answer. (A) (B) (C)
5. Mark your answer. (A) (B) (C)
6. Mark your answer. (A) (B) (C)
7. Mark your answer. (A) (B) (C)

Part 3 Conversations

04 T-CD 1-04

Listen to the conversation. Then choose the best answer to each question below.

8. What is the man's occupation?
   (A) Telephone operator
   (B) Internet salesman
   (C) Repairman
   (D) Customer-services assistant
   (A) (B) (C) (D)

9. Why did the woman make the call?
   (A) There is an error in her billing statement.
   (B) Her account has been canceled.
   (C) She needs to make an additional payment.
   (D) Her vacuum cleaner has not been delivered yet.
   (A) (B) (C) (D)

10. What does the woman need to do?
   (A) Go get a copy of the bill.
   (B) Call the man back as soon as possible.
   (C) Mail the bill to the man.
   (D) Return the vacuum cleaner back to the store.
   (A) (B) (C) (D)

Part 4 Talks

05 T-CD 1-05

You will hear a short talk. Choose the best answer to each question below.

11. How do we know the Japanese knife is so popular?
    (A) It is used by sushi chefs.
    (B) It is sold all over the world.
    (C) The factory can't keep up with demand.
    (D) The speaker recommends it.
    Ⓐ Ⓑ Ⓒ Ⓓ

12. What does the man mean when he says, "It's a little pricey"?
    (A) It is slightly heavy.
    (B) It is light and thin.
    (C) It is on sale.
    (D) It costs a little more.
    Ⓐ Ⓑ Ⓒ Ⓓ

13. Why can it be used for slicing raw fish as well as for cutting beef and chicken?
    (A) Because of its sharpness.
    (B) Because it is so beautiful.
    (C) Because it is so long.
    (D) Because it comes from Japan.
    Ⓐ Ⓑ Ⓒ Ⓓ

コーヒーブレーク

■リスニングのコツ(1)■

リスニングで高得点を獲得するには、音を聞くと同時に英文を理解するスキルが必要になります。そのためのトレーニング方法はいくつかありますが、ここでは「速聴」を紹介します。「速聴」とは、通常のスピードよりも速いスピードで聞くことで、脳の処理スピードや音声認知スピードを高速化させるトレーニング方法です。例えばリスニング教材を1.5倍速や2倍速に設定し、英文を繰り返し聞いてみましょう。1日15分でも構いません。普段からそのスピードに慣れておくと、通常スピードに戻したときに、英単語やチャンク(意味のかたまり)がより鮮明に、かつ驚くほどゆっくり聞こえるようになります。とはいえ、「速聴」に効果があるのは中級者以上と言われています。初級者はいきなり「速聴」を試すのではなく、まずは通常のスピードに慣れ、正確に英語の音を聞き取ることができるよう何度も練習して下さい。

Unit 2 Shopping (2)

Grammar Review 動詞（be 動詞・進行形・未来形）

1. John **is** an exchange student here in Japan from Australia, but he **is** back in Sydney for a few weeks now.
ジョンはオーストラリアから日本に来た交換留学生ですが、今、2～3週間、シドニーに戻っています。

2. My brother usually **gets** up at six, but he **overslept** today.
弟はふつう6時に起きるが、今日は寝坊した。

3. While **I'm doing** my homework at the desk, my cat **is lying** peacefully on my lap.
机で宿題をしている間、私のネコは膝の上で穏やかに眠っている。

4. Our client from Taiwan **is arriving** at Haneda Airport at 3 p.m. tomorrow.
台湾の顧客が明日、午後3時に羽田空港に到着します。

5. I **will** stay up late tonight and finish writing my term paper for history class.
今晩は徹夜して、歴史の授業の学期末レポートを書き終えるつもりです。

1. be 動詞の意味は主に①「～です」、②「～いる、ある」を表す。
2. 一般動詞は be 動詞以外の動詞を指し、動作・状態を表す。
3. 進行形 … be 動詞＋動詞の現在分詞（動詞～ ing）。
現在進行形① 現在の進行中の動作を表す。
4. 現在進行形② 未来の予定を表す。
5. 未来の時制① … 助動詞 will ＋動詞の現在形（意思未来・単純未来）
未来の時制② … be going to ＋動詞の現在形（未来の計画、根拠に基づいた判断）

Exercise 1

Choose the best word to complete each sentence below.

1. There (was, are, were) a larger audience at our products exhibition than we expected.
2. Every salesperson (do, does, done) his or her best to make a good showing.
3. Our flight (left, is leaving, leave) for Los Angeles early tomorrow morning.
4. While I (ride, was riding, rides) on my bike, it suddenly got a flat tire.
5. According to the weather report, it (rain, rained, is going to rain) heavily this evening.

Exercise 2

Match these key words or phrases from the Reading Comprehension section to their definitions below.

1. drill	2. directions	3. power supply	4. confirm	5. department

_____ (A) the electrical energy needed for lighting and heating

_____ (B) to provide proof for something or say that something is definitely true

_____ (C) information or instructions that tell people what to do and how to do it

_____ (D) a division of a company or other organization

_____ (E) a practice exercise that shows people how to act in case of earthquake, fire or other emergency

Part 5 Incomplete Sentences

T-CD 1-06

Choose the best answer to complete each sentence below.

1. The trendiest shopping area for young people in Tokyo is Shibuya, _____ the fashions and styles you see there influence all of Japan.
   (A) which
   (B) how
   (C) what
   (D) where
   Ⓐ Ⓑ Ⓒ Ⓓ

2. The Ginza shopping area is only _____ away.
   (A) a fifteen-minutes walk
   (B) fifteen minutes walk
   (C) fifteen minute's walk
   (D) a fifteen-minute walk
   Ⓐ Ⓑ Ⓒ Ⓓ

3. Our duty-free store currently _____ on numerous TV shows, in newspapers and online news sites.
   (A) is being featured
   (B) has featured
   (C) was featured
   (D) had been featuring
   Ⓐ Ⓑ Ⓒ Ⓓ

4. The bond that _____ among all the merchants by working together gives our shopping area its vitality.
   (A) did form
   (B) was forming
   (C) has formed
   (D) is formulated
   Ⓐ Ⓑ Ⓒ Ⓓ

5. As many as 1,200 bookstores may agree _____ convenience stores.
   (A) to tie up with
   (B) to do away with
   (C) to stand in for
   (D) to compete with
   Ⓐ Ⓑ Ⓒ Ⓓ

Part 6 Text Completion

T-CD 1-07

A word or phrase is missing in some of the sentences below. Four answer choices are given below each of those sentences. Select the best answer to complete the text.

Shopping

One of the icons of daily life in Japan is the local convenience store, ___6___ a "konbini" for short. For many Japanese people, convenience stores have ___7___ an essential part of their lives. Open 24 hours a day, konbini offer not only food but also many other goods and services that make life a little easier for young and old alike. The first convenience store ___8___ in Japan over fifty years ago; today, there are more than 50,000 of the handy little shops around the country. It is not unusual to ___9___ several konbini clustered around busy stations or intersections.

6. (A) called (B) meant
   (C) referred (D) regarded
   Ⓐ Ⓑ Ⓒ Ⓓ

7. (A) enjoyed (B) involved
   (C) made (D) become
   Ⓐ Ⓑ Ⓒ Ⓓ

8. (A) developed (B) came out
   (C) was introduced (D) was built
   Ⓐ Ⓑ Ⓒ Ⓓ

9. (A) confirm (B) see
   (C) look for (D) enter
   Ⓐ Ⓑ Ⓒ Ⓓ

Part 7 Reading Comprehension

T-CD 1-08

Choose the best answer for each question.

Notice

On Wednesday, October 15, just before noon, we will conduct an earthquake drill requiring the participation of all staff members. When the drill starts, all employees must immediately stop working and follow the directions of the announcement.

When you hear that an earthquake measuring magnitude 6 is in progress, drop to the floor and take cover under your desk. Get up only when it is announced that the shaking has stopped. Then, open your office room doors and follow the directions to make your way to the nearest exit. Do not use the elevators. During an earthquake, the power supply is often cut off, and the elevators may stop between floors. So use the staircases. Keep in mind that broken pieces of glass from overhead windows may fall and hurt you even after the shaking has stopped. So protect your head with your bag, a file, or other object.

After everyone has left the building, we will gather at Central City Park, to the north of our office. After your department manager takes the roll call and confirms everyone's safety, the drill will be finished.

10. What is the purpose of the notice?
    (A) To notify all staff members about a disaster prevention measure
    (B) To warn employees of an upcoming earthquake
    (C) To remind all staff members of the next meeting
    (D) To encourage all staff members to stop working overtime
    Ⓐ Ⓑ Ⓒ Ⓓ

11. Why should employees avoid taking the elevators?
    (A) The elevators will soon become overcrowded and dangerous to ride in.
    (B) An electrical blackout may occur and people may be trapped inside an elevator.
    (C) The elevators are reserved for bosses and executives.
    (D) The elevators are not conveniently located.
    Ⓐ Ⓑ Ⓒ Ⓓ

12. What is suggested that members do to maintain safety as they are escaping from the building?
    (A) They should keep calm and not run.
    (B) They should be careful where they step, because the passages will be covered with broken glass.
    (C) They should protect themselves from broken glass that may be falling from overhead.
    (D) They should hurry directly to Central City Park. Ⓐ Ⓑ Ⓒ Ⓓ

コーヒーブレーク

■リスニングのコツ（2）■

集中して音声を聞いた後に、少し遅れて音声を復唱（モノマネ）する「シャドーイング」もまた、リスニング力の向上が期待されます。「シャドーイング」には大きく分けて、英文を見ながら行う方法と英文を見ない（音声のみ）で行う方法がありますが、いずれの方法においても、事前に「シャドーイング」に使う教材の英単語や英文法を完全に理解しておく必要があります。はじめは理解しやすい簡単な英文で書かれた教材を使うのが良いでしょう。そして、それらの教材を使って、まずは英文を見ながら行う方法で、慣れてきたら、英文を見ないで行う方法で練習してみましょう。英文も少しずつ難しくしていきます。英文を見ないで行う方法で、教材の英文を正確に復唱できるようになった時、自身のリスニング力が向上していることを実感するはずです。

Unit 3 Food (1)

Useful Tips 発音・リスニング トレーニング

音の無声化

発音する時は喉（声帯）を通って空気を出していますが、この空気の出し方には２通りあります。
喉を震わせて出す音（有声音）と、喉を震わせない音（無声音）です。単語が有声音で終わり次の単語が無声音で始まる場合、前の有声音が無声音に変化することがあります。これを同化といいます。つまり、前の有声音が後ろの無声音にあわせて同じものに変化します。例えば、「of」/əv/ の後に無声音「c」で始まる「course」がくると、「of course」/əf kɔ́ːs/（英），/əf kɔ́ːrs/（米）になります。

（有声音）
of
/əv/

（無声音）
of course
/əf kɔ́ːs/（英）
/əf kɔ́ːrs/（米）

音の消失

単語の中の音が消えてしまうか、非常に弱く発音されることも多くあります。これを消失と呼びます。特に「t」の発音でよく見られます。
「fight」/fai(t)/

音の連結

front of：/frʌnt(ə)v/ のような音になります。前の語末の子音と、次の語頭の母音が連結して、一つながりに聞こえます。

Challenge

A. Choose the correct word from the box to complete each sentence below.

(a) exchanges	(b) warranty	(c) flour	(d) deposit	(e) foodstuff

1. Some people are allergic to white bread made from wheat (   ).
2. You place your money into a bank (   ), and the bank uses your funds to make loans to people and businesses.
3. This model has a three-year (   ) for the owner's protection.
4. The most common (   ) around the globe is, I think, rice.
5. No returns or (   ) are made unless the item is faulty or is not as described.

B. Choose the correct response to each question / statement on the left from among the responses on the right.

1. I need to stop eating such unhealthy foods.
2. What are you going to have along with your sandwich?
3. I'm so thirsty.
4. I could go for some fried chicken and French fries.
5. It won't take much time to make, I hope.

(a) I think I'll have a piece of fruit.
(b) I know what you mean. Me, too!
(c) So am I. Let's get something to drink.
(d) Not at all. Just a few minutes.
(e) That sounds delicious. I'll have the same.

Part 1 Photographs

06 T-CD 1-09

For each picture, you will hear four short statements. Look at the pictures below and choose the statement that best describes what you see in each picture.

1.

Ⓐ Ⓑ Ⓒ Ⓓ

2.

Ⓐ Ⓑ Ⓒ Ⓓ

Part 2 Question-Response

07 T-CD 1-10

Choose the best response to each question or statement you hear.

3. Mark your answer. (A) (B) (C)
4. Mark your answer. (A) (B) (C)
5. Mark your answer. (A) (B) (C)
6. Mark your answer. (A) (B) (C)
7. Mark your answer. (A) (B) (C)

Part 3 Conversations

08 T-CD 1-11

Listen to the conversation. Then choose the best answer to each question below.

8. What type of event is being organized?
   (A) A directors' meeting
   (B) A retirement dinner
   (C) A trade show
   (D) A party
   (A) (B) (C) (D)

9. Look at the graphic below. What option has the man most likely chosen?
   (A) The Japanese snack platter
   (B) The fried chicken and roast beef combo
   (C) The beefsteak dinner
   (D) The seafood assortment
   (A) (B) (C) (D)

Special Menu

Assorted Japanese snack foods	$550
Fried chicken & roast beef combination	$650
Beef cooked in tomato base and garden salad	$700
Seafood variety	$750

10. What information does the man still have to provide?
   (A) A list of attendees' names
   (B) A cash deposit
   (C) Payment details
   (D) His company's address
   (A) (B) (C) (D)

Part 4 Talks

09 T-CD 1-12

You will listen to a short talk. Choose the best answer to each question below.

11. What type of store is Andy's?

(A) A small convenience store
(B) A clothing store
(C) A grocery store
(D) A discount shop

Ⓐ Ⓑ Ⓒ Ⓓ

12. How often is this sale held?

(A) Every weekend
(B) Once a month
(C) Twice a year
(D) Once a year

Ⓐ Ⓑ Ⓒ Ⓓ

13. How can customers get an additional discount?

(A) By mentioning where they heard about the sale
(B) By registering for the in-store prize draw
(C) By buying more than ten items
(D) By presenting a special coupon

Ⓐ Ⓑ Ⓒ Ⓓ

コーヒーブレーク

■リスニングのコツ(3)■

I know a girl who was walking in the park yesterdayという英文があるとしましょう。この英文を読んで、時間をかけて理解するのは決して難しいことではありません。しかし、その英文を聞いて即座に理解するためには、例えばI know a girlが聞こえたら「私は女の子を知っている」、who was walkingが聞こえたら「歩いていた」、in the parkが聞こえたら「公園で」、yesterdayが聞こえたら「昨日」、というように、聞こえた順番に理解していくスキルが必要です。そのためには文全体を把握した後、後ろから訳して理解しようとせず、普段から英文を前から理解するよう心掛けて下さい。この方法を習得することができれば英文読解の速度も格段にあがります。また、はじめのうちは、英語を日本語に訳しながら理解してしまうかもしれませんが、慣れれば日本語に訳すことなく、英語を英語のまま理解することも可能です。

Unit 4 Food (2)

Grammar Review

受動態（受け身）

1. English **is** now **taught** at most primary schools in Japan.
今、英語は日本のほとんどの小学校で教えられています。

2. Has the flight to Boston **been delayed** due to the stormy weather?
嵐のため、ボストン行きの便は遅れているのですか。

3. Our opening ceremony **will be held** in Tokyo next month.
来月、東京で私どもの開店祝賀会が開催されます。

4. The efficiency of Japanese eco-cars **is known to** people all over the world.
日本のエコカーの効率性は、世界中の人々に知られている。

5. Many fans **were thrilled with** her wonderful, gold medal-winning performance at the Olympics.
多くのファンが、オリンピックで金メダルを取った彼女のすばらしい演技にぞくぞくした。

1. 受動態…be 動詞＋動詞の過去分詞（＋ by ～）
主語が動作を行なう場合を能動態、動作を受ける場合を受動態という。
2. 受動態の疑問文。受動態の否定文・疑問文は、be 動詞の否定文・疑問文の場合と同じ。
3. 助動詞を使った受動態…助動詞＋ be 動詞＋動詞の過去分詞
4. by を使わない受動態…be covered with、be filled with など。
5. 感情を表す受動態…日本語では能動態でも英語では受動態になる。be surprised at、be pleased with など。

Exercise 1

Choose the best word to complete each sentence below.

1. The company presidency was not (took, taken, take) over by the eldest son of the retiring president.
2. Do you remember who (did, is, was) transferred to our London branch last year?
3. Our factory's excellent quality-control system must (maintain, be maintained, maintaining).
4. The vacancy for chief editor will be filled (on, at, by) the most qualified applicant.
5. All the company's executives were disappointed (to, with, for) last month's sales figures.

Exercise 2

Match these key words or phrases from the Reading Comprehension section to their definitions below.

1. fit	2. procedure	3. COD	4. policy	5. out of stock

____ (A) collect (or cash) on delivery

____ (B) to be the right size or shape for a person to wear

____ (C) a way of doing something or a plan of action, officially followed by an organization

____ (D) in a shop or warehouse, not having goods available for sale or distribution

____ (E) a formal or correct way of doing something

Part 5 Incomplete Sentences

T-CD 1-13

Choose the best answer to complete each sentence below.

1. It is not certain exactly when tofu (bean curd) _____ to Japan.

   (A) made up
   (B) was introduced
   (C) was found
   (D) invaded

   Ⓐ Ⓑ Ⓒ Ⓓ

2. Foods are neatly _____ according to categories such as canned goods, flour, rice, beverages, and condiments.

   (A) shelved
   (B) stood
   (C) contributed
   (D) purchased

   Ⓐ Ⓑ Ⓒ Ⓓ

3. Natto (fermented soybeans) _____ the ingredient (soya) that forms the basis of many traditional Japanese foods.

   (A) consists of
   (B) makes up
   (C) is made from
   (D) is made of

   Ⓐ Ⓑ Ⓒ Ⓓ

4. There is nothing I like better than pancakes that are _____ maple syrup and melted butter.

   (A) served as
   (B) cooked in
   (C) equipped with
   (D) served with

   Ⓐ Ⓑ Ⓒ Ⓓ

5. Our ad agency is to create a role for Napa sparkling wine as a luxury drink ____ on special occasions.

   (A) to be enjoyed
   (B) for enjoyed
   (C) to have been enjoyed
   (D) enjoying

   Ⓐ Ⓑ Ⓒ Ⓓ

Part 6 Text Completion

T-CD 1-14

A word or phrase is missing in some of the sentences below. Four answer choices are given below each of those sentences. Select the best answer to complete the text.

Food

Rice is one of the world's most essential crops. About half of the global population ___ (6) rice as a major source of nutrition. The recent decoding of rice's genome sequence should speed up conventional rice crossbreeding programs. The process to develop a new and better variety of rice and pass it on to farmers ___ (7) to take only three years to realize. For example, a new strain of rice was ___ (8) in Iwate Prefecture in 2016. The new rice, which was ___ (9) "Konjiki-no-kaze"(Wind of Gold), has found great favor among consumers. The rice has a somewhat stickier texture than other varieties and a mildly fragrant flavor. Many say that "Konjiki-no-kaze" is one of the best rice strains in Japan.

6. (A) depends on (B) is used to (C) introduces (D) have — Ⓐ Ⓑ Ⓒ Ⓓ

7. (A) is determined (B) is wished (C) is expected (D) is valued — Ⓐ Ⓑ Ⓒ Ⓓ

8. (A) featured (B) differentiated (C) decided (D) developed — Ⓐ Ⓑ Ⓒ Ⓓ

9. (A) expressed (B) dubbed (C) considered (D) judged — Ⓐ Ⓑ Ⓒ Ⓓ

Part 7 Reading Comprehension

T-CD 1-15

Choose the best answer for each question.

To: Customer Service
From: Joseph Dunn
Date: February 14
Subject: Returns

Dear Customer Service,

On February 11, I ordered several items from your website store. They just arrived today, so I tried each item on to see if it fit. I'm afraid the black sweater I ordered is a little tight for me. Could you replace it with a larger one? I have ordered some polo shirts from your website before. These items fit me perfectly, and I am very satisfied with them. They were all medium-sized shirts, so the black sweater I ordered was the same size. I like the design and the color of the sweater very much, so all I want is to get a larger one. My order number is MS1979009, which includes these other purchased goods: one jacket and two pairs of jeans. How can I return the sweater? Please let me know your procedure for returning goods.

Sincerely,
Joseph Dunn

To:	Joseph Dunn
From:	Roger Smith
Date:	February 15
Subject:	Re: Returns

Dear Mr. Dunn,

Thank you for shopping at our website store. Of course you can return the item that doesn't fit you. All you have to do is repackage the item and send it back to us COD. If you have any questions, please visit our website, where our return policy is explained in detail.

We are very sorry, but the larger sweater you requested is out of stock right now. If you are interested in a larger one in white or brown with the same design, we will send one as soon as we receive your return. If not, we will cancel your sweater order, and you will not be charged for the item. We look forward to your reply.

Sincerely,

Roger Smith
Customer Service Manager
Ellis Fashion Company

10. What items did Mr. Dunn buy from the website store this time?
    (A) A black sweater, one jacket, and two pairs of jeans
    (B) A black sweater, some polo shirts, and a pair of jeans
    (C) A jacket, a shirt, and several other items
    (D) A black sweater and a jean jacket

Ⓐ Ⓑ Ⓒ Ⓓ

11. What does Mr. Dunn want to do?
    (A) He wants to return all the items he purchased.
    (B) He wants to send back the sweater because it is too small.
    (C) He wants to send back the sweater because he doesn't like the design.
    (D) He wants to return the sweater because it is the wrong color.

Ⓐ Ⓑ Ⓒ Ⓓ

12. What is Mr. Dunn asked to do to return the item?

(A) Keep the item until a delivery person comes to collect it.
(B) Pay an extra shipping cost.
(C) Return the item COD.
(D) Return the item in person.

Ⓐ Ⓑ Ⓒ Ⓓ

13. What does the manager suggest that Mr. Dunn should do?

(A) The manager suggests that he should wait for the larger black sweater to be delivered.
(B) The manager suggests that he should buy a larger sweater in another color.
(C) The manager suggests that he cancel the order because the sweater is no longer being produced.
(D) The manager suggests that he should order a similar sweater from another website.

Ⓐ Ⓑ Ⓒ Ⓓ

コーヒーブレーク

■ 英語の発音について ■

冒頭の「TOEIC® Listening & Reading Test について」で述べたように、TOEIC®のリスニング問題はアメリカ英語、カナダ英語、イギリス英語、オーストラリア英語、ニュージーランド英語で発音されます。そのため、リスニングで高得点を獲得するためには、インターネットで各国のニュースサイトを聞くなど、普段から事前にこれらの国の訛りに慣れておく必要があります。TOEIC® ではこの5ヶ国の英語しか発音されません。しかし、世界ではこれらの英語以外にそれぞれの国がそれぞれの訛りある英語で自信を持ってコミュニケーションをとっています。皆さんがこの5ヶ国で話されているような発音を目指すのは構わないですが、それらの発音ができないからと言って特に気にする必要はありません。ただ、相手に意味が通じないような発音は、コミュニケーションが成立しないため問題ですね。

Unit 5 Family (1)

Useful Tips　発音・リスニング　トレーニング

発音の簡略化

簡略化（reduction）とは、スペリング上は発音されるべき音が、脱落または弱化することを言います。例えば、Good night. という挨拶のフレーズは Goo’ nigh’ というように、語尾の破裂音が省略されます。

（例）Get back. ⇒ Ge’ ba’　　handbag ⇒ han’ba’　　Let it go. ⇒ Let i’ go.

音の脱落

単語の末尾の子音と次の語頭の子音が（ほぼ）同じ音の時に、前の子音が脱落したり、非常に弱く発音されたりして、聞こえにくくなります。例えば、Good day は /gúd dei/ とはならず、/gú’dei/ という風に聞こえます。

（例）big game ⇒ 前の g が脱落して /bi’géim/ と聞こえます。
　　put together ⇒ 前の t が脱落して /pu’təgéðər/ と聞こえます。

他に「子音で終わる単語」+「似た子音で始まる単語」の場合にも同様に前の子音が脱落します。

（例）good time ⇒ 前の d が脱落して /gú’taim/ と聞こえます。

Challenge

A. Choose the correct word or phrase from the box below to complete each of these sentences.

(a) around	(b) members	(c) warmth	(d) treasure	(e) family friends

1. I could feel the (　　　　　　) of my homestay family.
   私はホームステイ先の家族の温かさを感じることができました。
2. I really (　　　　　　) the time I spend with my family.
   私は家族との時間をとても大切にします。
3. We are (　　　　　　) with the Adamses.
   私たちはアダムズ家とは家族ぐるみのお付き合いです。
4. How many (　　　　　　) are there in your family?
   あなたは何人家族ですか。
5. I'll be home by (　　　　　　) 6 p.m.
   6時頃には家に戻ります。

B. Choose the correct response to each question / statement on the left from among the responses on the right.

1. Let me make something clear to you.
2. Do you look like anyone in your family?
3. Can I have a hamburger for lunch, Mom?
4. Where does your family go on a vacation each year?
5. What do you do when you get home from school each day?

(a) People say I look just like my older sister.
(b) We usually visit Hokkaido every summer.
(c) I usually do my homework first.
(d) What is it?
(e) Sure, I'll make it right now.

Part 1 Photographs

10 T-CD 1-16

For each picture, you will hear four short statements. Look at the pictures below and choose the statement that best describes what you see in each picture.

1. 

(A) (B) (C) (D)

2. 

(A) (B) (C) (D)

Part 2 Question-Response

11 T-CD 1-17

Choose the best response to each question you hear.

3. Mark your answer. (A) (B) (C)
4. Mark your answer. (A) (B) (C)
5. Mark your answer. (A) (B) (C)
6. Mark your answer. (A) (B) (C)
7. Mark your answer. (A) (B) (C)

Part 3 Conversations

12 T-CD 1-18

Listen to the conversation. Then choose the best answer to each question below.

8. What are the speakers talking about?
   (A) The man's health
   (B) The man's appearance
   (C) The man's school
   (D) Today's weather

Ⓐ Ⓑ Ⓒ Ⓓ

9. What does the woman give the man?
   (A) A tissue
   (B) A glass of water
   (C) Some medicine
   (D) His health insurance card

Ⓐ Ⓑ Ⓒ Ⓓ

10. What does the woman suggest that the man do?
   (A) Take the day off
   (B) Make a doctor's appointment
   (C) Get up and hurry to school
   (D) Change the medicine he takes

Ⓐ Ⓑ Ⓒ Ⓓ

Part 4 Talks

13 T-CD 1-19

You will hear a short talk. Choose the best answer to each question below.

11. Where is this announcement being made?
   (A) At an exhibition
   (B) In a furniture store
   (C) In an office
   (D) In a science museum

Ⓐ Ⓑ Ⓒ Ⓓ

12. What type of products does Thomas and Johnson carry?
   (A) Fitness equipment
   (B) Mobile phones
   (C) Kitchen appliances
   (D) Water coolers

Ⓐ Ⓑ Ⓒ Ⓓ

13. What does the speaker say about the on-line catalog?

(A) It includes an invitation to the exhibition.
(B) It offers a 10% discount on washing machines.
(C) It offers very low prices to customers who use it.
(D) Its copies are available at the Thomas and Johnson booth.

Ⓐ Ⓑ Ⓒ Ⓓ

コーヒーブレーク

ブレーズ・パスカル (Blaise Pascal; 1623-1662)。仏の哲学者

I have made this letter longer than usual only because I have not had the time to make it short.
私はこの手紙を普段より長めにしたが､それは単に短くする時間がなかったからだ。

この引用はパスカルの著作集 (1657) の中にあり、後世の作家によく用いられています。オリジナルのフランス語は、Je n’ai fait celle-ci plus longue que parce que je n’ai pas eu le loisir de la faire plus courte.ですが、これを文字通り英訳すると I have made this longer than usual because I have not had time to make it shorter. となります。仏語も英語も共に “letter” の文字が欠落していますが、それは元々のフランス語の記述が手紙なので、あえて “letter” の意味を入れる必要がなかったからです。逆に翻訳する時はこの背景を知り、人々に理解してもらえるように、“letter” という言葉を添える必要があります。文法の学習としてこの引用を if-clause にしてみれば、If I had had more time, I would have written a shorter letter. となります。いわゆる「仮定法過去完了」の表現です。

Unit 6 Family (2)

Grammar Review

完了形

1. **I've** not **finished** my work yet, so I'm going to have to work overtime today.
まだ仕事が終わっていないので、今日は残業しなければいけません。

2. Millions of overseas tourists **have visited** Akihabara since the 2000s began.
2000 年代が始まってからずっと、何百万もの海外の旅行者が秋葉原を訪れた。

3. **Have** you **ever worked** part-time at a convenience store?
今まで、コンビニでアルバイトをしたことがありますか。

4. I realized that I **had left** my smartphone on the train.
列車にスマートフォンを忘れたことに気が付いた。

5. By the time we see it, the Buddhist image that was designated as a national treasure **will have been exhibited** for over a month.
私達が見る時まで、国宝として指定されたその仏像は、一ヶ月以上展示されます。

1. 現在完了形…have (has) ＋動詞の過去分詞
現在完了形は現在を基準に、過去に起こった出来事が現在にまで関係している場合に使われる。1 の例文は現在完了の完了・結果。just、already などと共に使われる。

2. 現在完了形の継続。since（過去の一時点）、for（期間）などと共に使われる。

3. 現在完了形の経験。ever（疑問文の場合）、never などと共に使われる。

4. 過去完了形…had ＋動詞の過去分詞

5. 未来完了形…will ＋ have ＋動詞の過去分詞

Exercise 1

Choose the best word to complete each sentence below.

1. Our new marketing campaign (have, is, has) already proved successful.
2. I (have made, make, made) a presentation for our clients last Friday.
3. We have already (discuss, been discussing, discussing) our new project in the conference room for two hours!
4. When I arrived at the bus stop, the bus (have, had, will have) already left.
5. By the time I make my next business trip to Hong Kong, I (will have, have, had) visited the city more than a dozen times.

Exercise 2

Match these key words from the Reading Comprehension section to their definitions below.

1. assure	2. vehicle	3. sight	4. locate	5. arrange

____ (A) to establish or find in a particular place

____ (B) to make sure something will happen by making preparations for it

____ (C) a machine like a car or truck used for transporting goods or people on land

____ (D) to tell someone that something will surely happen or be all right

____ (E) famous or interesting places that are often visited by tourists

コーヒーブレーク

ワシントン・アーヴィング (Washington Irving; 1783-1859)。米国の作家

Great minds have purpose, others have wishes.
偉大な人たちは目的を持ち、そうでない人たちは願望を持つ

名詞 "wish" の類義語には "dream"、"desire" などがあり、結果を出すことよりも単に「夢」を抱くことに比重があります。一方、"purpose" の類義語には "goal"、"aim" などがあり、明確な成果を前提とします。建国後間もない 1800 年代のアメリカ。多言語話者として知られる作家アーヴィングは、「人種のるつぼ (melting pot; salad bowl)」となった将来の American "minds" の姿を既に心に描いていたのかもしれません。

Part 5 Incomplete Sentences

T-CD 1-20

Choose the best answer to complete each sentence below.

1. My father _____ ill for a week when the doctor was finally sent for.
   (A) had been
   (B) was
   (C) has been
   (D) was being
   Ⓐ Ⓑ Ⓒ Ⓓ

2. If it doesn't clear up by tomorrow, it _____ for six days.
   (A) is raining
   (B) rains
   (C) has been raining
   (D) will have been raining
   Ⓐ Ⓑ Ⓒ Ⓓ

3. I'll watch television when I _____ my work.
   (A) will do
   (B) have finished
   (C) have been doing
   (D) begin
   Ⓐ Ⓑ Ⓒ Ⓓ

4. By next Christmas, my family _____ here for seven years.
   (A) has lived
   (B) was living
   (C) will have been living
   (D) lives
   Ⓐ Ⓑ Ⓒ Ⓓ

5. Yuzuru Hanyu _____ superstar status before the Winter Olympics in 2018.
   (A) has already achieved
   (B) already achieved
   (C) was already achieving
   (D) had already achieved
   Ⓐ Ⓑ Ⓒ Ⓓ

Part 6 Text Completion

T-CD 1-21

A word or phrase is missing in some of the sentences below. Four answer choices are given below each of those sentences. Select the best answer to complete the text.

Family (Eco-houses)

Eco-houses are habitats that are truly healthy environments for human beings to live in. What's more, eco-houses are environmentally sustainable: they ___**6**___ to conserve essential resources like water and electricity and to recycle whenever possible. Today's eco-house models are also very attractive and perfectly comfortable. As incidences of "sick-house syndrome" rise, more and more people are ___**7**___ to suspect that much modern housing is harmful to their health. Sick-house syndrome ___**8**___ when people live with indoor pollutants like mold, dust, or harmful chemicals. In addition, the recent rise in the number of allergy cases ___**9**___ to this harmful syndrome.

6. (A) are designed (B) are kept
   (C) are found (D) are decided
   Ⓐ Ⓑ Ⓒ Ⓓ

7. (A) wondering (B) thinking
   (C) beginning (D) doubting
   Ⓐ Ⓑ Ⓒ Ⓓ

8. (A) causes (B) lessens
   (C) sustains (D) develops
   Ⓐ Ⓑ Ⓒ Ⓓ

9. (A) had attributed (B) has been attributed
   (C) attributes (D) is attributing
   Ⓐ Ⓑ Ⓒ Ⓓ

Part 7 Reading Comprehension

T-CD 1-22

Choose the best answer for each question.

To: Helen Adler
From: Mycroft Baker
Date: April 20
Subject: Hotels

Dear Ms. Adler,

Thank you for visiting us and booking your ticket for a round-trip flight to Milan. This is Mr. Phelps's first visit to Milan, and I assure you that he will truly enjoy his stay there. It's a beautiful place! When you booked the flight yesterday, you asked me to give you the names of some of the hotels our agency recommends. I have picked out a few hotels that I think will meet your expectations. Please have a look at the attached file.
By the way, we will also provide Mr. Phelps with transportation from Milano Malpensa Airport to your hotel. There are a train and a shuttle-bus service that operate between the airport and the downtown area, but these services take more time than the service we offer. And not only is our service faster: you can get to your hotel directly from the airport more cheaply than if you were to take a taxi, and you can sit back and enjoy a comfortable ride in our luxury vehicle. If you have any questions, please don't hesitate to call me.

Sincerely,

Mycroft Baker
Strand Travel Agency

The Hotels in Milan that we highly recommend

The Grand Hotel ...... located near Milano Malpensa Airport; most convenient for flights; includes continental breakfast

The Milano Hotel ...... located in the downtown area, really easy to visit famous sights and get to the railway station; popular with short-stay tourists; but the area is a little noisy even late at night

The Tourist Inn ...... located in a quiet area; a 10-minute walk away from downtown, but with a fine view of a beautiful park; friendly and helpful staff; includes bread and coffee breakfast

The Hotel Da Vinci ...... located in the suburbs; most suitable for long-stay visitors; has an indoor pool and a highly rated Italian restaurant; staff capable of providing multilingual services; includes buffet style breakfast

To:	Mycroft Baker
From:	Helen Adler
Date:	April 21
Subject:	Re: Hotels

Dear Mycroft Baker,

Thank you for your e-mail and hotel recommendations. I'm afraid I cannot give you our final decision right now, because Mr. Phelps is out of the office. As soon as he gets back, we'll choose from among your recommendations. I can't say for sure, but I think he will choose the one located in the center of the city (the Milano Hotel). I forgot to ask you to make sure that a dependable high-quality WiFi service is available. Are these hotels all OK for that? Mr. Phelps complained about the trouble he had with the WiFi service at the hotel he stayed at in Paris. I know most hotels in large cities these days provide a reliable WiFi service, but please make sure the service is good enough to use in any room and at any time without any problems. By the way, could you arrange for Mr. Phelps to get a seat at La Scala? He is a long-time opera lover and is eager to attend a performance there after his business negotiations have wound up. Could you please let us know what is being performed at La Scala during Mr. Phelps's stay in Milan? Thank you again for all your help.

Sincerely,

Helen Adler
St Clair Textile Company

10. Why does Mr. Baker recommend the agency's transportation service?
   (A) Because it's quicker than going by train or bus.
   (B) Because it is safer than other transportation services.
   (C) Because the train and the shuttle-bus services are often out of order.
   (D) Because it is difficult to catch a taxi at the airport. Ⓐ Ⓑ Ⓒ Ⓓ

11. Which hotels will Mr. Phelps most likely NOT choose?
   (A) The Tourist Inn and the Hotel Da Vinci
   (B) The Grand Hotel and the Milano Hotel
   (C) The Milano Hotel and the Tourist Inn
   (D) The Grand Hotel and the Hotel Da Vinci Ⓐ Ⓑ Ⓒ Ⓓ

12. What, most likely, is Helen Adler's job?
   (A) She is a travel agent.
   (B) She is an office intern.
   (C) She is Mr. Phelps's secretary.
   (D) She is an accountant. Ⓐ Ⓑ Ⓒ Ⓓ

13. What trouble did Mr. Phelps have in Paris?
   (A) He had problems with the digital devices in his hotel room.
   (B) He had a difficult time getting downtown from the airport.
   (C) He couldn't sleep well because the neighborhood was so noisy.
   (D) The staff at the front desk were rude and inefficient. Ⓐ Ⓑ Ⓒ Ⓓ

14. What is the main purpose of Mr. Phelps's visit to Milan?
   (A) To take a short vacation from the office
   (B) To visit the sights of the city
   (C) To meet and discuss business with clients
   (D) To attend a famous opera performance Ⓐ Ⓑ Ⓒ Ⓓ

Unit 7 Music (1)

Useful Tips 発音・リスニング　トレーニング

冠詞 (article)、"a/an" と "the" の発音について

a：「不定冠詞」(indefinite article) と呼ばれ、単数の可算名詞に用いられます。"a" は母音 (aeiou ＝ア行) の前では "an" に変わります。例えば、an American car「アメリカ製の車」のように。また、a euro「ユーロ」、a one-way ticket「片道切符」では、"an" を思わず使いたくなります。決めては「文字」ではなく「音」にあります。"a" と "an" の区別は、"aeiou" の「文字」ではなく、"アエイオウ" の「音」がポイントです。先に示した EU (European Union･ヨーロッパ連合) の通貨 "euro" も "e" で始まりますが、発音は /e/ ではなく /jˈʊ/ です。従って、"a euro" となります。

［例］He has **an** uncle called Charlie.
(彼にはチャーリーという名のおじさんがいる。)
He has **a** generous uncle.
(彼には気前の良いおじさんがいる。)

the：「定冠詞 (definite article)」と呼ばれ、単数／複数、可算／不加算にかかわらず用いられます。普段は /ðə/ と発音しますが、aeiou の音の前では /ði/ に変わります。

［例］I've just read **the** article on **the** Internet.
(ちょうどその記事をインターネット上で読んだところです。)

Challenge

Choose the correct word from the box to complete each sentence below.

(a) book	(b) mood	(c) playing	(d) supposed	(e) seeing

Woman: How about taking in a concert next weekend?

Man: Great idea. What do you feel like (1)?

Woman: Bubu Rock is (2). How about that band?

Man: Actually, I'd prefer something a little more mellow. I'm not in the (3) for that kind of loud, upbeat music.

Woman: What do you suggest, then?

Man: I'm not sure. Let's check the web and see what's on.

Woman: How about Lovelove? Their music is (4) to be really nice.

Man: Sounds perfect. Let's (5) two seats right now.

Part 1 Photographs

14 T-CD 1-23

For each picture, you will hear four short statements. Look at the pictures below and choose the statement that best describes what you see in each picture.

1. 

Ⓐ Ⓑ Ⓒ Ⓓ

2. 

Ⓐ Ⓑ Ⓒ Ⓓ

Part 2 Question-Response

15 T-CD 1-24

Choose the best response to each question or statement you hear.

3. Mark your answer. Ⓐ Ⓑ Ⓒ

4. Mark your answer. Ⓐ Ⓑ Ⓒ

5. Mark your answer. Ⓐ Ⓑ Ⓒ

6. Mark your answer. Ⓐ Ⓑ Ⓒ

7. Mark your answer. Ⓐ Ⓑ Ⓒ

Part 3 Conversations

16 T-CD 1-25

Listen to the conversation. Then choose the best answer to each question below.

8. What has the woman done so far?
   (A) Made the seat reservations
   (B) Renewed her membership
   (C) Visited the theater where the musical is playing
   (D) Listened to some orchestra music

Ⓐ Ⓑ Ⓒ Ⓓ

9. What kind of seats will she get?

(A) Near the back
(B) In the Orchestra section
(C) Whatever's available
(D) Back stage

Ⓐ Ⓑ Ⓒ Ⓓ

10. How will she pay for the seats?

(A) In cash
(B) By credit card
(C) With a bank check
(D) Using a coupon

Ⓐ Ⓑ Ⓒ Ⓓ

Part 4 Talks

17 T-CD 1-26

You will hear a short talk. Choose the best answer to each question below.

11. What is this announcement concerned with?

(A) The serious effects of pneumonia
(B) The price of concert tickets
(C) Trips to Europe and Canada
(D) The cancellation of a music tour

Ⓐ Ⓑ Ⓒ Ⓓ

12. What should ticket holders do with their tickets?

(A) Return them to the place where they bought them
(B) Try to attend the concert anyway
(C) Visit Alice Wander in the hospital to ask for a refund
(D) Sell their tickets to other loyal fans

Ⓐ Ⓑ Ⓒ Ⓓ

13. What has Alice Wander promised?

(A) To never get pneumonia again
(B) To cancel all her upcoming performances
(C) To contact all her fans and apologize directly
(D) To recover in good health and become a better singer

Ⓐ Ⓑ Ⓒ Ⓓ

Unit 8 Music (2)

Grammar Review

不定詞

1. Japan's stated current objective is **to promote** tourism. Thus it is important for the government **to increase** the number of inbound tourists.
表明された日本の現在の目標は観光産業を促進することである。だから、政府が外国人旅行者数を増やすことが重要である。

2. What is the best way **to market** our new high-tech product?
我が社のハイテク新製品を売り出すための最も良い方法は何だろうか。

3. I am really glad **to have passed** the examinations and **to get** the credits I need for graduation.
試験に合格して卒業に必要とする単位が取れて私は本当にうれしい。

4. **Needless to say**, don't post overly personal and private information on social networking sites.
言うまでもないが、ソーシャルネットワーキングサイトに行き過ぎた個人のプライベート情報を載せるな。

5. Our manager in the Sales Department **makes** us **work** very hard to meet the established sales targets.
営業部のマネージャーは、定められた販売目標を達成するために私たちをとても懸命に働かせます。

1. 不定詞…to ＋動詞の原形
名詞的用法…不定詞が主語・補語・目的語になる。

2. 形容詞的用法…不定詞が形容詞として名詞を修飾したり、補語になる。

3. 副詞的用法…不定詞が動詞、形容詞、副詞、文全体を修飾する。

4. 独立不定詞として、慣用的に使われる。to begin with、so to speak など。

5. 使役の動詞（have、let、make）＋目的語＋動詞の原形～「目的語に～させる」
知覚動詞（see、hear など）＋目的語＋動詞の原形～「目的語が～するのを見る（聞く）」

Exercise 1

Choose the best word to complete each sentence below.

1. Lack of expertise in overseas business makes it difficult for us (enter, to enter, entered) the global market.
2. Could you give me something (to write, writing, written) with?
3. Michael worked most industriously, aiming (becoming, to become, became) a manager faster than any other staff member.
4. (Making, To make, Made) matters worse, I had my hands full dealing with complaints from our overseas customers.
5. Welcome! Let me (checking, to check, check) your passport and flight confirmation.

Exercise 2

Match these key words from the Reading Comprehension section to their definitions below.

1. surgery	2. deterioration	3. condolence	4. discreet	5. colleague

_____ (A) sympathy expressed for someone whose loved one or friend has died

_____ (B) a person you work with in a business or other place

_____ (C) a state of developing into a worse physical condition

_____ (D) invasive medical treatment of disease or injury by repairing or removing affected parts of the body

_____ (E) careful or thoughtful about what one says or does

Part 5 Incomplete Sentences

T-CD 1-27

Choose the best answer to complete each sentence below.

1. Mary went on _____ conducting under a prominent maestro.
   (A) to succeed
   (B) to teach
   (C) to study
   (D) to influence
   Ⓐ Ⓑ Ⓒ Ⓓ

2. The best way to enjoy karaoke is to choose a song _____ your voice.
   (A) to perform
   (B) to suit
   (C) to sound
   (D) to understand
   Ⓐ Ⓑ Ⓒ Ⓓ

3. It was Seiji Ozawa himself who helped _____ close ties to our local school.
   (A) assess
   (B) introduce
   (C) consider
   (D) establish
   Ⓐ Ⓑ Ⓒ Ⓓ

4. Our music teacher often asked the maestro _____ a quartet for our class.
   (A) to conduct
   (B) to name
   (C) to present
   (D) to express
   Ⓐ Ⓑ Ⓒ Ⓓ

5. It is imperative for young musicians to train themselves _____ each voice on its own.
   (A) to be able to hear
   (B) to have hearing for
   (C) to hear of
   (D) to hear from
   Ⓐ Ⓑ Ⓒ Ⓓ

Part 6 Text Completion

T-CD 1-28

A word or phrase is missing in some of the sentences below. Four answer choices are given below each of those sentences. Select the best answer to complete the text.

Music

The Only Flower in the World is a hit song by one of Japan's most popular singing groups. ___6___ the adoring fans of one of the group's members was a girl suffering from a serious lung disease. When the singer (one of the members) heard about the girl, he ___7___ her a special visit in the hospital. His kind words of support, it is said, gave her the hope and courage ___8___, and from that day on, she began to recover. What better story than this ___9___ the genuine healing power of music in our lives?

6. (A) Among (B) About
   (C) Within (D) Inside
   Ⓐ Ⓑ Ⓒ Ⓓ

7. (A) had (B) made
   (C) paid (D) brought
   Ⓐ Ⓑ Ⓒ Ⓓ

8. (A) to breathe (B) to live
   (C) to accept (D) to think
   Ⓐ Ⓑ Ⓒ Ⓓ

9. (A) to ensure (B) to emerge
   (C) to generate (D) to illustrate
   Ⓐ Ⓑ Ⓒ Ⓓ

Part 7 Reading Comprehension

T-CD 1-29

Choose the best answer for each question.

Dear Mrs. Brand,

All of the staff members of our department were shocked and saddened to hear about Edmund's untimely death. When we heard he was in the hospital to have surgery, we were all worried about him. But then we were relieved to hear that his surgery had been successful and hoped that he would recover quickly and return to work with us soon. So the sudden deterioration of his condition and subsequent death came as a shock and source of great sadness and regret. Please accept our deepest condolences.

Edmund's death is a great loss to our department — and our company. He was a wonderful colleague, always cheerful and discreet at the office. Though he was so busy and had his hands full of important work to do, he always thought of other staff members. He was always willing to take the time to help his colleagues and give them helpful advice when they were having trouble at work. He was truly loved and respected by us all.

Mrs. Brand, if there is anything we can help you with, please do not hesitate to let us know.

Sincerely yours,

Peter Reginald

Sales Manager

Baker Publishing Inc.

10. Why did Mr. Brand's death come as such a shock?
   (A) Because his physical condition had seemed to get worse.
   (B) Because he had never had any regular health problems before.
   (C) Because the operation he had had been a success and indicated full recovery.
   (D) Because his illness was so serious and a quick recovery could not be expected.
   Ⓐ Ⓑ Ⓒ Ⓓ

11. What is the main purpose of the letter?
   (A) To inform Mrs. Brand of her husband's death
   (B) To make inquiries about the cause of the death of Mrs. Brand's husband
   (C) To express all the staff members' regret for the death of a respected colleague like Mr. Brand
   (D) To list Mr. Brand's many achievements as a sales person
   Ⓐ Ⓑ Ⓒ Ⓓ

12. What was Mr. Brand like?
   (A) As much as possible, he kept to himself in the office.
   (B) He was a reliable colleague who was often asked for advice by his co-workers.
   (C) Being ill, he was contemplative and hard to talk to.
   (D) He was a strict manager and always finding fault with the people he worked with.
   Ⓐ Ⓑ Ⓒ Ⓓ

コーヒーブレーク

ヘンリー・デイビッド・ソロー (Henry David Thoreau; 1817-1862)。米国の作家

It is not enough to be busy; so are the ants. The question is: What are we busy about?
忙しいだけでは十分ではない。アリだって忙しい。問題は、何をしていて忙しいのかということだ。

私たちは本当にやるべき大切なこと、常に実のあることに対して時間を使いたいものです。これに関連して、例えばルイス・キャロル (Lewis Carroll; 1832-1898) の『不思議の国のアリス』にはその冒頭、白ウサギが登場します。「ああ、大変だ！遅刻してしまいそう」と言って、チョッキのポケットから時計を取り出し、時間を確認する場面があります。時間は捉え方によって蛇腹のように長くなったり、短くなったりします。往々にして私達は「忙しい、忙しい」が口癖になっていますが、実はそれは思い込みである場合が多いのです。Time is money. 時間を有効に使いたいものです。

Unit 9 Amusement (1)

Useful Tips　発音・リスニング　トレーニング

得点アップのためには聞き取りミスを減らすこと。

① 音が似ている場合

The man is walking in the park.（彼は公園を歩いている。）
The man is working on a crossword puzzle.（彼はクロスワードパズルをやっている。）

The woman is looking at the grass.（女性は芝生を見ている。）
The woman is looking at the glass.（女性はガラスを見ている。）

② 動作と状態

The man is putting on a coat.（男性はコートを着ようとしている。）動作
The man is wearing a coat.（男性はコートを身につけている。）状態

③ その他、よく似た単語

fold（折る）・hold（持つ）
floor（床）・flower（花）
car（車）・cart（カート）
here（ここ）・hair（髪）
truck（トラック）・track（跡；コース）

⇒ Part 1. Photographs 2 の写真を参考に

Part1 の写真問題は、写っていないものは選ばない。

① 写真に写っていないものは選ばない

細部が問われることはほぼありません。目立ったものに目を向けましょう。

② 位置情報をとらえる。（位置関係を表す前置詞）

in front of ～「～の前に」
side by side「隣り合って」
upside down「逆さまに」
stacked / piled「積み重なった」
arranged / lined up「置かれた」
in a row / line「一列に」

Challenge

Choose the correct word or phrase from the box to complete each sentence below.

(a) intermission	(b) discount tickets	(c) next to each other
(d) silent mode	(e) same-day tickets	

1. (   ) are available at the coupon booth.
   割引切符は割引き券売り場で入手できる。
2. (   ) may be sold out.
   当日券は売り切れかもしれない。
3. The seats are (   ).
   席は隣同士です。
4. Put your smartphones in (   ) as a courtesy.
   マナーとしてスマートフォンを消音設定にする。
5. The audience can get drinks during the (   ).
   幕間に観客は飲み物をとることができる。

Part 1 Photographs

18 T-CD 1-30

For each picture, you will hear four short statements. Look at the pictures below and choose the statement that best describes what you see in each picture.

1.

Ⓐ Ⓑ Ⓒ Ⓓ

2. 

(A) (B) (C) (D)

Part 2 Question-Response

19 T-CD 1-31

Choose the best response to each question or statement you hear.

3. Mark your answer. (A) (B) (C)

4. Mark your answer. (A) (B) (C)

5. Mark your answer. (A) (B) (C)

6. Mark your answer. (A) (B) (C)

7. Mark your answer. (A) (B) (C)

Part 3 Conversations

20 T-CD 1-32

Listen to the conversation. Then choose the best answer to each question below.

8. Where does this conversation take place?
   (A) At home
   (B) In a park
   (C) In the zoo
   (D) In a restaurant

(A) (B) (C) (D)

9. Who is Amy?

(A) She is a babysitter.
(B) She is the speakers' neighbor.
(C) She is the speakers' daughter.
(D) She is the speaker's mother.

Ⓐ Ⓑ Ⓒ Ⓓ

10. At what time will they most likely arrive at the zoo?

(A) 10:00
(B) 10:30
(C) 12:30
(D) 14:00

Ⓐ Ⓑ Ⓒ Ⓓ

Part 4 Talks

21 T-CD 1-33

You will listen to a short talk. Choose the best answer to each question below.

11. What kind of announcement is this?

(A) An advertisement for an amusement park
(B) A cancellation notice
(C) A weather forecast
(D) A traffic report

Ⓐ Ⓑ Ⓒ Ⓓ

12. Where is Geordieland Amusement Park located?

(A) Just off the A3 motorway
(B) In downtown Newcastle
(C) Right at junction 14
(D) On the outskirts of Newcastle

Ⓐ Ⓑ Ⓒ Ⓓ

13. Who is able to get a discount for Geordieland?

(A) Anyone who goes as part of a family group
(B) Anyone who is 65 or older
(C) Children 12 years old and under
(D) Anyone who buys a ticket on the Internet

Ⓐ Ⓑ Ⓒ Ⓓ

Unit 10 Amusement (2)

Grammar Review

分詞

1. The gold-medal winner's figure skating was really **exciting**. His **excited** fans threw lots of bouquets onto the skating rink after his performance.
   金メダリストのフィギュア・スケートは本当にわくわくさせた。演技の後、彼の興奮したファンたちは、たくさんの花束をリンクに投げ込んだ。
2. The anticancer drug **developed** recently is full of promise for people suffering from the disease.
   最近、開発された抗ガン剤は、その病気に苦しむ人にとってかなり有望です。
3. **Watching** a video on YouTube on the sofa last night, I fell asleep.
   昨晩、ソファで YouTube の動画を見ていたら、寝てしまった。
4. After experiencing some trouble, we **had** our factory machinery carefully **examined** by a professional.
   何らかの故障を経験した後、専門家に工場の機械を綿密に検査してもらった。
5. I **had** my wallet **stolen** on a packed train this morning.
   今朝、満員電車の中で、財布を盗まれた。

1 分詞は現在分詞と過去分詞に分かれる。分詞が 1 語の時は、名詞の前から修飾する。

2. 他の語句と結びついた分詞が、名詞の後ろから修飾する場合。

3. 分詞構文は分詞が文全体を修飾し、時・理由・条件等を表す。

4. have＋目的語＋過去分詞① 使役（「～してもらう」）

5. have＋目的語＋過去分詞② 被害（「～される」）

Exercise 1

Choose the best word to complete each sentence below.

1. When a breeze blows, (coloring, colored, color) leaves from maple trees fall more easily than those that have not turned color yet.
2. Don't leave your computer (running, ran, run) all day long, especially when you expect to leave your desk for a long time.
3. The lecture and Question-Answer session will begin at 4 p.m., (following, followed, follow) by an informal reception and refreshments.
4. (See, Seeing, Seen) from the top of Tokyo Sky Tree, all the buildings and houses below look almost like toys.
5. Could you call the facilities section to have the air conditioning (fixed, fix, fixing) in this office?

Exercise 2

Match these key words or phrases from the Reading Comprehension section to their definitions below.

1. firm	2. grateful	3. financial assistance	4. book	5. tip

____ (A) to keep or reserve something for use at a particular time in the future

____ (B) a useful or practical piece of advice about how to do something better

____ (C) feeling thanks or having the desire to show one's gratitude

____ (D) support given to somebody who needs money, usually for university study

____ (E) a company or agency dedicated to business or a profession

Part 5 Incomplete Sentences

T-CD 1-34

Choose the best answer to complete each sentence below.

1. Offering people a wide range of nighttime entertainment options _____ as the key to success.
   (A) is viewed
   (B) is looked
   (C) is dealt
   (D) is revised
   Ⓐ Ⓑ Ⓒ Ⓓ

2. Spending on entertainment _____ to culture, sports, and recreation accounts for around one percent of overall purchases.
   (A) engaged
   (B) related
   (C) involved
   (D) appealed
   Ⓐ Ⓑ Ⓒ Ⓓ

3. With very few exceptions, one famous theme park will feature the same or very similar attractions that are _____ in all other theme parks.
   (A) attended
   (B) played
   (C) shown
   (D) found
   Ⓐ Ⓑ Ⓒ Ⓓ

4. Karaoke is an interesting activity for tourists to Japan to do, especially those _____ indoor entertainment.
   (A) opposed to
   (B) following on
   (C) looking for
   (D) associating with
   Ⓐ Ⓑ Ⓒ Ⓓ

5. "I've nothing else to do on my days off," the young man said while _____ "Pokemon Go."
   (A) acting
   (B) playing
   (C) searching
   (D) performing
   Ⓐ Ⓑ Ⓒ Ⓓ

Part 6 Text Completion

T-CD 1-35

A word or phrase is missing in some of the sentences below. Four answer choices are given below each of those sentences. Select the best answer to complete the text.

Amusement

On July 22, 2016, Pokemon fans in Japan were able to grab their smartphones and ____ (6) outdoors in pursuit of monsters as the new game "Pokemon Go" made its debut. "Pokemon Go," ____ (7) reality game that is free to download and play, uses a phone's GPS sensor and camera to guide players around streets and parks in their quest to find and capture Pokemon monsters. Under a sponsorship agreement, the roughly 2,900 McDonald's outlets in Japan became spots ____ (8) as Gyms and PokeStops, which means that McDonald's Japan is likely to enjoy healthy profits from the game. The video game industry has ____ (9) out a permanent niche in the world of entertainment.

6. (A) make up (B) move out
   (C) scatter over (D) set off
   Ⓐ Ⓑ Ⓒ Ⓓ

7. (A) an augmented (B) an inner
   (C) a fantastic (D) a hyper
   Ⓐ Ⓑ Ⓒ Ⓓ

8. (A) valued (B) known
   (C) respected (D) called
   Ⓐ Ⓑ Ⓒ Ⓓ

9. (A) discovered (B) tried
   (C) carved (D) taken
   Ⓐ Ⓑ Ⓒ Ⓓ

Part 7 Reading Comprehension

T-CD 1-36

Choose the best answer for each question.

To: consulting staff
From: Chiaki Furuya
Date: May 8
Subject: Reservation

Dear consulting staff,

I currently work part-time for a construction firm, and I have recently become very interested in studying about historical buildings and architecture at a university in Europe. I am looking for a course that is taught in English. I visited your website and noticed that your staff is very helpful for people who are seeking advice about studying abroad. I searched the Internet, and I have come up with a few colleges I hope to apply for. Though I know it greatly depends on the country and the college, I need to know as accurately as possible how much money my study abroad will cost, including living costs. And I would like to get a good scholarship, so I'd be grateful for your advice regarding financial assistance. Could I reserve a consultation with you for a week from today at around 6 p.m.? I can leave my office early on Wednesdays. I look forward to your reply.

Sincerely yours,

Chiaki Furuya

To:	Chiaki Furuya
From:	Jane Hamilton
Date:	May 9
Subject:	Re: Reservation

Dear Ms. Furuya,

Thank you for your request for a consultation reservation. I'm very sorry, but the time you requested for next Wednesday has already been booked. How about on Wednesday of the following week? Would that work for you? I'm confident that our experienced staff will be able to give you some very useful information and meet your expectations fully. If that day is all right with you, I'll book you a slot for 6:00 p.m. But please let me know ASAP if the day and time are acceptable.
By the way, we are planning to hold a consultation conference for all persons interested in studying abroad. Attendees can hear stories of the experiences of returnees who have just got back from abroad and can also talk to them in a casual setting. Some of them have earned a Ph.D. successfully and will provide attendees with helpful tips. If this sounds like something you would be interested in taking part in, please visit our website and check out the latest information about the conference.
We look forward to helping you and are awaiting your reply.

Sincerely,

Jane Hamilton
Consulting Staff Manager
ABC Consulting Agency

10. What does Ms. Furuya most probably do?

(A) She is a manager at a consulting agency.
(B) She is a temporary, part-time worker at a construction company.
(C) She is an architect's intern.
(D) She is a returnee student. Ⓐ Ⓑ Ⓒ Ⓓ

11. What advice would probably be the most useful to her?

(A) Advice about where to find the names of universities abroad
(B) Advice about financial matters, living expenses and scholarships
(C) Advice about foreign language study programs
(D) Advice on foreign Ph. D. programs Ⓐ Ⓑ Ⓒ Ⓓ

12. When will Ms. Furuya most likely have a consultation with the ABC staff?

(A) On May 22nd at around 6 p.m.
(B) On May 15th at around 6 p.m.
(C) On May 29th at around 6 p.m.
(D) On June 5th at around 6 p.m. Ⓐ Ⓑ Ⓒ Ⓓ

13. Why is Jane Hamilton encouraging Ms. Furuya to attend the consultation conference?

(A) Because it will give Ms. Furuya a chance to get useful information.
(B) Because she can receive a good scholarship if she attends.
(C) Because she can meet other returnees like herself.
(D) Because all conference attendees are guaranteed a place in a foreign college. Ⓐ Ⓑ Ⓒ Ⓓ

コーヒーブレーク

ウィリアム・ジェームズ（William James; 1842-1910）。米国の哲学者

Act as if what you do makes a difference. It does.
自分の行動が変化をもたらすかのごとく行動しなさい。それが変化をもたらすのだ。

イディオムとして as if ～「まるで～のように」があることはわかります。では、makes に三人称単数の "s" があることに気づきましたか？ what you do の部分は wh- 名詞節で、これを「it」又は「that」に置き換えれば文全体の構造が見えてきます。したがって、動詞の make には "s" が付きます。さらに、It does の後に省略されているものは、make a difference です。今度は前に does があるので、make には "s" が付きません。単語の配列はまるで「たすき掛け」のようにクロスして、言葉に安定感を与えています。

Unit 11 Pubs (1)

Useful Tips リスニング　内容理解　トレーニング

Part2 応答問題の得点アップはパターンに慣れること

① 重複ワードは選ばない。

Where is the inquiry **office**?（案内所はどこですか？）
(A) No, not at all.（いいえ、そんなことないです。）
(B) I went to my **office**.（自分のオフィスに行きました。）
(C) It's across the street.（通りを越えたところにあります。）

Where という疑問詞から場所について答える選択肢を選べばよいので、正解は (C) となります。Part2 の多くの場合、設問文と同じ語句、あるいは似た音の語句が入った選択肢は不正解となります。

② 単語から連想させる関連語が入っている。

How was the new restaurant on Baker Street?
(A) It was very crowded.（とても混雑していました。）
(B) No, it's too old.（いいえ、それはとても古いです。）
(C) The restroom is over there.（トイレは向こうにあります。）

正解は (A) となります。発話文の new、restaurant に対してそれぞれ old、restroom のような何かしら関連性のある音の響きやイメージを醸し出す語が対置され、受験者を惑わすことが多くあります。

Challenge

A. Choose the correct word or phrase from the box to complete each sentence below.

(a) recommend	(b) not included in	(c) crispy	(d) know	(e) occupied

1. The service charge is (   ) the check.
サービス料は勘定に含まれていない。
2. All the tables by the window are (   ).
窓側の席はすべてふさがっている。
3. Let me (   ) when you're ready.
用意が出来たら教えてください。
4. May I have (   ) bacon, please.
カリカリに焼いたベーコンをください。
5. What do you (   )?
お薦めはなんですか？

B. Rearrange the words and phrases below to make a complete sentence.

1. go to the counter / when / your number / please / on the right / is called
自分の番号が呼ばれたら右側のカウンターに行ってください。

....

2. this credit card / the expiration date / has / on / passed / already
このクレジットカードの有効期限はすでに過ぎています。

....

Part 1 Photographs

22 T-CD 2-1

For each picture, you will hear four short statements. Look at the pictures below and choose the statement that best describes what you see in each picture.

1. 

Ⓐ Ⓑ Ⓒ Ⓓ

2. 

Ⓐ Ⓑ Ⓒ Ⓓ

Part 2 Question-Response

23 T-CD 2-2

Choose the best response to each question or statement you hear.

3. Mark your answer. Ⓐ Ⓑ Ⓒ

4. Mark your answer. Ⓐ Ⓑ Ⓒ

5. Mark your answer. Ⓐ Ⓑ Ⓒ

6. Mark your answer. Ⓐ Ⓑ Ⓒ

7. Mark your answer. Ⓐ Ⓑ Ⓒ

Part 3 Conversations

24 T-CD 2-3

Listen to the conversation. Then choose the best answer to each question below.

8. What can be said about the Taj Mahal?
   (A) Its menu is limited.
   (B) Their prices are quite high.
   (C) It doesn't have a website.
   (D) The restaurant opened only recently. Ⓐ Ⓑ Ⓒ Ⓓ

9. Why won't the speakers go to Capri?
   (A) Because it's too far away.
   (B) Because it's closed today.
   (C) Because it's too expensive.
   (D) Because it's too spicy. Ⓐ Ⓑ Ⓒ Ⓓ

10. Where are the speakers going to eat tonight?
   (A) At an Indian restaurant
   (B) At an Italian restaurant
   (C) At a pub
   (D) They're going to stay home. Ⓐ Ⓑ Ⓒ Ⓓ

Part 4 Talks

25 T-CD 2-4

You will listen to a short talk. Choose the best answer to each question below.

11. On what day of the week will the upcoming pub quiz take place?
    (A) Thursday
    (B) Friday
    (C) Saturday
    (D) Sunday

Ⓐ Ⓑ Ⓒ Ⓓ

12. What will the team that comes in second in the quiz win?
    (A) Cash
    (B) A free glass of beer
    (C) A bottle of good wine
    (D) A ticket to the next pub event

Ⓐ Ⓑ Ⓒ Ⓓ

13. What is the maximum number of people that can be part of a pub quiz team?
    (A) 2 people
    (B) 6 people
    (C) 8 people
    (D) 10 people

Ⓐ Ⓑ Ⓒ Ⓓ

コーヒーブレーク

現代では、英語は世界共通言語（リンガ・フランカ）と言えますが、ヨーロッパの歴史で英語が公用語として使われたのは、そんなに古いことではありません。そもそもヨーロッパの公用語としての役割を果たしてきたのは、ラテン語であり、次はフランス語、そして英語という順番になります。ラテン語はもちろん、古代ローマ帝国の言語であり、近代まで、キリスト教聖職者階級、知識人層にとっては、国が違っても、ラテン語でコミュニケーションを取ることができたわけです。英語とは直接的な系統関係にはありませんが、フランス語を経由したものも含めると、英単語のかなりの数がラテン語に由来します。学生の皆さんにとって身近なラテン語起源の英単語に study があります。これはラテン語の動詞 studeo「〜に専心する」や、その名詞形 studium「努力」に由来します。語源から明らかなように、そもそも勉強とは、努力するものだということがわかりますね。

Unit 12 Pubs (2)

Grammar Review

動名詞

1. **Opening** the attached files of dubious e-mails may allow malware to infect your computer, so you should avoid **clicking** on the file.
疑わしい E メールの添付ファイルを開くと、マルウェアがコンピューターに感染するのを許すことになるかもしれません。だから、ファイルのクリックを避けるべきです。
2. I'm looking forward to **hearing** from you soon.
すぐにあなたからの連絡があるのを楽しみに待っています。
3. I was born in Japan, but I am ashamed of my **not knowing** very much at all about Japanese traditional culture.
私は日本に生まれましたが、日本の伝統文化について全く知らず恥ずかしい。
4. We are very proud of **our son's getting** a scholarship to Oxford University.
私たちは、息子がオックスフォード大学への奨学金を手に入れたことをとても誇りに思います。
5. I **remember** as a child **sending** a fan letter to my favorite professional baseball player.
子供のころ、大好きなプロ野球選手にファンレターを送ったことを覚えている。

1. 動名詞…動詞＋～ ing「～すること」。動名詞は名詞として、主語・補語・目的語となる。例文 1 は動名詞が主語と目的語として使われている。動名詞を目的語に取る動詞には、enjoy、finish 等がある。不定詞を目的語に取る動詞には、want、decide 等がある。
2. 動名詞を使った慣用表現。How about ～ ing?、feel like ～ ing など。
3. 動名詞の否定文。not が動名詞の前に置かれる。
4. 動名詞の意味上の主語。動名詞の動作を表す主語は、代名詞の場合は、目的格か所有格、名詞の場合は、そのままの形か所有格。
5. 動詞の目的語として、動名詞と不定詞の両方を取れる動詞のうち、forget をはじめ、意味の異なる動詞がある。
比較 Please **remember to send** a Christmas card to all our regular customers.
（全ての常連客にクリスマスカードを送るのを忘れないで下さい。）

Exercise 1

Choose the best word to complete each sentence below.

1. He got upset and left the office without (say, saying, said) good-bye.
2. After (call, calls, calling) my client, I realized my mistake and called him right back to make an apology.
3. Most of my colleagues have stopped (smoking, to stop, smoked) successfully.
4. Our company's logo is meant (to represent, representing, represented) "well-being."
5. I'll never forget (making, to make, made) an exclusive contract with the world-famous rock-and-roll star, my first big success as an agent.

Exercise 2

Match these key words from the Reading Comprehension section to their definitions below.

1. catering	2. appreciate	3. questionnaire	4. install	5. favorable

_____ (A) of something pleasant, good or desirable

_____ (B) the job of providing food and drinks at a party or other event

_____ (C) a survey to be answered in writing by many people

_____ (D) to thank someone politely for something he or she has done

_____ (E) to put in a piece of equipment somewhere so that it is ready for use

Part 5 Incomplete Sentences

T-CD 2-5

Choose the best answer to complete each sentence below.

1. Most pubs focus on _____ beers, ales and similar drinks.
   (A) distributing
   (B) donating
   (C) offering
   (D) developing
   Ⓐ Ⓑ Ⓒ Ⓓ

2. In addition to _____ for the needs of tourists, inns traditionally acted as community gathering places.
   (A) had been providing
   (B) provided
   (C) being provided for
   (D) providing
   Ⓐ Ⓑ Ⓒ Ⓓ

3. The practice _____ hops to the production of beer was introduced in the early 15th century.
   (A) of adding
   (B) for increasing
   (C) of growing
   (D) of requiring
   Ⓐ Ⓑ Ⓒ Ⓓ

4. Japan's climate has always made _____ grapes for wine a challenge.
   (A) using
   (B) growing
   (C) harvesting
   (D) ripening
   Ⓐ Ⓑ Ⓒ Ⓓ

5. In 2007, Japan Airlines (JAL) began _____ its passengers wine made in Japan.
   (A) advertising
   (B) sampling
   (C) serving
   (D) featuring
   Ⓐ Ⓑ Ⓒ Ⓓ

Part 6 Text Completion

T-CD 2-6

A word or phrase is missing in some of the sentences below. Four answer choices are given below each of those sentences. Select the best answer to complete the text.

Pub

Japanese sake is an alcoholic beverage made by _____ 6 rice that has been polished to remove the bran. The process is somewhat similar to that of _____ 7 beer. The polished rice is cooked in boiling water until it becomes a mash. Koji, an enzyme, is added to the mash to convert the starch in the rice to sugar. By _____ 8 yeast, the sugar is then converted to alcohol through the fermentation process. In brewing beer, in contrast, these changes from starch to sugar and from sugar to alcohol occur as two consecutive steps. But in sake _____ 9, the changes occur simultaneously.

6. (A) introducing (B) converting
   (C) spoiling (D) fermenting
   Ⓐ Ⓑ Ⓒ Ⓓ

7. (A) marketing (B) making
   (C) consuming (D) constructing
   Ⓐ Ⓑ Ⓒ Ⓓ

8. (A) adding (B) engaging
   (C) involving (D) decreasing
   Ⓐ Ⓑ Ⓒ Ⓓ

9. (A) changing (B) shifting
   (C) brewing (D) distinguishing
   Ⓐ Ⓑ Ⓒ Ⓓ

Part 7 Reading Comprehension

T-CD 2-7

Choose the best answer for each question.

— Notice —

Dear Staff Members of the Sales Department, Carter Chemical Company Ltd.

Thank you for your continued use of our catering service. We have recently begun providing a new service — a rental coffee machine for offices. As part of our promotional campaign, we are offering this new service to you for free for one week and hope that good regular customers like you will give the new service a try. If you do, we would appreciate it if you would evaluate our new service by completing the questionnaire sheets attached to the machine. — [1] — The service description is as follows:

Office Coffee Service!

Users can enjoy far more delicious — and authentic — coffee than they can at cafés, fast-food restaurants, or convenience stores. Moreover, one cup costs less than 1 dollar, which means a big saving. We offer a wide variety of coffee flavors: special blend, mocha, espresso, café au lait, cocoa, and many others! What's more, the machine is super easy to use. Just put a pod of the flavor you like in the machine, place your cup under the spout and push the button. That's all there is to it! In less than 60 seconds, your delicious cup of coffee is ready to enjoy! And the machine requires very little maintenance! — [2] — So why not give our great-tasting coffee a try? You have nothing to lose!

Sincerely,

Berkeley & Crispin Catering Company

Berkeley & Crispin Catering Company Questionnaire

(1) How would you evaluate our coffee's taste?

Excellent ☐ Good ☑ Fair ☐ Poor ☐

(2) What flavor do you like best?

Café au lait

(3) If this machine were installed in your office, would you use it?

Yes ☑ No ☐

(4) If you answered "Yes" to question (3), how often would you use it per week?

More than 15 times

(5) What flavor would you add to our selection?

nothing

(6) What improvements would you suggest we make to our coffee machine and service, if any?

— Thank you for giving me this great coffee experience. For such delicious coffee, the price is really reasonable. If it were installed here, I would use it every day. — [3] — One thing, though: I'm afraid that sometimes the coffee was not as hot as I like it.

— Notice —

Dear Staff Members of the Sales Department, Carter Chemical Company Ltd.

Thank you for trying our coffee and taking the time to respond to our questionnaire. We really appreciated getting answers from more than two-thirds of your staff. We're happy to report that nearly all of the 36 respondents liked our new service. Your honest comments for the improvement of our service have been of great help. One, in particular, really surprised us—that the coffee was not always as hot as it should be. We are now making every effort to find out why our machine does not always serve coffee at the same high temperature. But rest assured: we will soon solve this problem and serve our customers the hottest, tastiest coffee available anywhere—at the best possible price. — [4] — We hope you will give us the opportunity to provide you with our improved service.

Sincerely,

Berkeley & Crispin Catering Company

10. What is NOT a selling point of this coffee service?
    (A) The large variety of flavors it offers
    (B) The reasonable price per cup of coffee
    (C) The machine's attractive and compact design
    (D) The delicious taste of the coffees offered

Ⓐ Ⓑ Ⓒ Ⓓ

11. What complaint was made in the questionnaire?
    (A) The coffee often tastes weak and bland.
    (B) The machine didn't offer the person's favorite flavor of coffee.
    (C) The coffee is sometimes lukewarm.
    (D) The machine is not user-friendly.

Ⓐ Ⓑ Ⓒ Ⓓ

12. Approximately how many staff members are there in the Sales Department?
   (A) 34
   (B) 44
   (C) 54
   (D) 64
   Ⓐ Ⓑ Ⓒ Ⓓ

13. What is the cause of the problem with the coffee maker?
   (A) The thermometer doesn't function properly.
   (B) The hot water overflows the cup.
   (C) The problem has not yet been identified.
   (D) The power supply often shuts down.
   Ⓐ Ⓑ Ⓒ Ⓓ

14. In which of the positions marked [1], [2], [3], and [4] does the following sentence best fit?

   "We assure you that you will never have to worry about spills."

   (A) [1]
   (B) [2]
   (C) [3]
   (D) [4]
   Ⓐ Ⓑ Ⓒ Ⓓ

コーヒーブレーク

本や映画の邦題が、原題と違っている場合がありますね。例えば映画では、主題歌と共に大ヒットしたディズニー映画『アナと雪の女王』の原題は *Frozen*（凍った）、『塔の上のラプンツェル』は *Tangled*（もつれあった）なので、直訳では、イメージがかなり違ってしまうでしょう。名作小説の中には、邦題で定着したものもあります。オールコットの『若草物語』の原題は *Little Women*（幼い女性たち）ですが、作品の雰囲気が伝わります。秀逸の邦題は、サリンジャーの『ライ麦畑で捕まえて』でしょうか。原題の *Catcher in the Rye* を直訳すると「ライ麦畑の捕手」となり、野球小説と勘違いされてしまいそうですね。日本文学も英語圏に翻訳されますが、*The Three-Cornered World* は何だかわかりますか。正解は、夏目漱石の『草枕』です。原題とはかけ離れていますが、作品世界をうまく言い表していますね。

Unit 13 Countryside (1)

Useful Tips リスニング 内容理解 トレーニング

Part3 & Part4 のコツ

① 音声と設問の順序は概ね一致します。例えば、設問 1 は音声の前半、設問 2 は中盤、設問 3 は音声の最後にヒントが出ることが多いようです。

Good afternoon passengers. (Q1) This is the pre-boarding announcement for flight AB089 to London, Heathrow. (Q2) We are now inviting passengers with small children and passengers requiring special assistance, as well as first-class and executive-class passengers, to begin boarding at this time. Please have your boarding pass and passport ready. (Q3) Regular boarding for Economy-class will begin in approximately fifteen minutes. Economy-class boarding will be done according to passenger seat number. Thank you.

Q1: Where does this talk take place?
⇒ airport をイメージする 空港の出発ゲートで聴くアナウンス

Q2: Who is going to get priority boading?
⇒ 優先搭乗のアナウンス

Q3: When will the airplane take off?
⇒ エコノミークラス搭乗完了後だから少なくとも 15 分以上かかる

② 音声を聴く前に設問と選択肢を先読みして、問われる内容、ジャンルから背景を思い描きます。

【頻出のジャンル】
telephone message（留守番電話） recorded message（自動音声メッセージ）
talk（対話） announcement（アナウンス） news report（ニュース）
radio broadcast（ラジオ放送）等

③ 集中できない時は目をつぶり、視覚情報を遮断して音声のみから会話場面を思い描きます。

④ マークシートはちょい塗り程度にして、リスニングに集中します。塗りつぶすのは Part5 以降の解答中にします。

Challenge

A. Choose the correct phrase from the box to complete each sentence below.

(a) cut down on	(b) fossil fuel	(c) organic farming
(d) global warming	(e) carbon footprint	

1. (　　　　　　　) prices shot through the roof.
   化石燃料の値段が急騰しました。
2. We'll make every effort to reduce our (　　　　　　　).
   私たちは二酸化炭素排出量を減らすあらゆる努力をします。
3. I'm worried about the (　　　　　　　) trend.
   私は地球の温暖化傾向を心配しています。
4. We can try to (　　　　　　　) our energy consumption.
   私たちはエネルギーの節約をすることができます。
5. (　　　　　　　) is a sustainable eco-friendly operation.
   有機農法は自然に優しい方法です。

B. Rearrange the words below to make a complete sentence.

1. recommend / you / can / to visit / places / some / good ?
   訪問するのにどこか良い所を紹介してくれませんか？

2. benefits / other / any / the / do / tickets / include ?
   チケットには何か特典が付いているのですか？

Part 1 Photographs

26 T-CD 2-8

For each picture, you will hear four short statements. Look at the pictures below and choose the statement that best describes what you see in each picture.

1. 

Ⓐ Ⓑ Ⓒ Ⓓ

2. 

Ⓐ Ⓑ Ⓒ Ⓓ

Part 2 Question-Response

27 T-CD 2-9

Choose the best response to each question or statement you hear.

3. Mark your answer. Ⓐ Ⓑ Ⓒ

4. Mark your answer. Ⓐ Ⓑ Ⓒ

5. Mark your answer. Ⓐ Ⓑ Ⓒ

6. Mark your answer. Ⓐ Ⓑ Ⓒ

7. Mark your answer. Ⓐ Ⓑ Ⓒ

Part 3 Conversations

28 T-CD 2-10

Listen to the conversation. Then choose the best answer to each question below.

8. What are the speakers doing?
   (A) Hiking in a forest
   (B) Parking a car
   (C) Hunting for bears
   (D) Visiting a zoo
   Ⓐ Ⓑ Ⓒ Ⓓ

9. Who are the speakers?
   (A) A teacher and a student
   (B) Two co-workers
   (C) A tour guide and a tourist
   (D) A father and daughter
   Ⓐ Ⓑ Ⓒ Ⓓ

10. If they see a bear, what does the man advise that they do?
   (A) Get back into the car
   (B) Run away as fast as they can
   (C) Put their backpacks on the ground and walk backwards away from the bear
   (D) Make a loud noise and run towards the bear to scare it away
   Ⓐ Ⓑ Ⓒ Ⓓ

Part 4 Talks

29 T-CD 2-11

You will hear a short talk. Choose the best answer to each question below.

11. Who is speaking?
    (A) A parent
    (B) A farmer
    (C) A zoo keeper
    (D) A teacher

Ⓐ Ⓑ Ⓒ Ⓓ

12. What's the first activity of the day?
    (A) Having lunch
    (B) Washing vegetables
    (C) Watching the farmer milk the cows
    (D) Feeding the small animals

Ⓐ Ⓑ Ⓒ Ⓓ

13. What's the last activity of the day?
    (A) Washing vegetables
    (B) Harvesting vegetables
    (C) Milking the cows
    (D) Going to the toilet

Ⓐ Ⓑ Ⓒ Ⓓ

コーヒーブレーク

明治以降、探偵小説というジャンルは英米から輸入されて確立しましたが、今や名探偵という存在は、マンガやアニメでもお馴染みと言えるでしょう。そのため、detectiveという単語を聞くと、「私立探偵」を思い浮かべる方が多いのでは？一般に「刑事」の意味でも使われるので、注意が必要。また、イギリスの探偵小説を読むと、制度の違いに当惑する方も多いのでは？変死が起きた場合は、まるで裁判のようなinquest（検死審問）が開かれ、事故死なのか殺人なのか、公の判断がくだされます。弁護士はbarrister（法廷弁護士）とsolicitor（事務弁護士）に分かれ、法廷で弁論を行うのは、barrister、事務手続きはsolicitorとなります。依頼人から事件を依頼されるのはsolicitorの方であり、solicitorがbarristerに法廷での弁論を依頼します。日本人にとってはややこしいですね。

Unit 14 Countryside (2)

Grammar Review

前置詞

1. A: You know that the deadline for our paper is 3 p.m. **on** Friday, right?
   B: Yes, I know. Why don't we go to the library and work on it now? It's open **till** 10 p.m. So it's still open now.
   A: レポートの締め切りが金曜日の午後３時なの知ってるよね？
   B: うん、知ってるよ。図書館に行って、今、取り組まない？午後10時まで開いてるんだ。だから今、まだ空いてるよ。

2. I bumped into an old college classmate of mine **at** Shinjuku Station a few days ago, so we had a drink **at** a bar **in** the station.
   数日前、新宿駅で、大学の頃の旧友にばったり出くわしたので、駅の飲み屋で一杯飲んだ。

3. Our boss leaves **for** San Francisco on a business trip this evening, and a local staff member is going to meet him at the airport.
   今晩、上司は出張でサンフランシスコに向かい、地元のスタッフが空港に出迎えに行く。

4. I was going to take the train to City Hall, but I carelessly left my wallet at the office. So I had no money to buy a ticket **with** at the station.
   電車で市役所に行こうと思ったが、うっかり財布を会社に忘れてしまった。だから、駅で切符を買うお金がなかった。

5. **In case of** a fire, don't panic. Calmly walk to the nearest fire exit.
   火事の場合、パニックになってはいけない。落ち着いて一番近い火災用非常口に歩いて行きなさい。

1. 時を表す前置詞 … in、at、on、by、till、until、for、during、through など。
2. 場所を表す前置詞 … in、at、on、by、above、over、under、below など。
3. 方向を表す前置詞 … for、to など。
4. 方法、手段、道具を表す前置詞 … by、with など。
5. 群前置詞 … 2語以上の語が結合して、1つの前置詞の働きをする。because of「～のために」、instead of「～の代わりに」など。

Exercise 1

Choose the best word to complete each sentence below.

1. We had been receiving more and more orders for our new smartphone (during, for, on) several months and were especially busy (during, for, on) the week before Christmas.
2. Could you give me a hand moving that office cabinet (with, on, at) your left and help me put it (in, on, at) that corner over there?
3. I intended to go to the office (by, in, for) my car, but the traffic report said the roads were heavily congested, so I went (by, in, for) subway instead.
4. According (for, to, at) the latest consumer report, our new eco-car is rated the most environment-friendly of all those introduced this year.
5. I'll be in charge (of, to, at) this project while our manager is away on business.

Exercise 2

Match these key words and phrases from the Reading Comprehension section to their definitions below.

1. office supplies	2. personnel	3. apologize	4. fault	5. meet

_____ (A) to say that you are sorry for having done something bad or wrong

_____ (B) the people who are employed in an organization such as a company

_____ (C) to satisfy something that is required

_____ (D) stationery products that are used by businesses, schools, and so on

_____ (E) the responsibility or blame for some error or problem

Part 5 Incomplete Sentences

T-CD 2-12

Choose the best answer to complete each sentence below.

1. You can enjoy lush nature _____ the fullest and step into the world of folktales in the countryside.
   (A) for
   (B) on
   (C) to
   (D) by
   Ⓐ Ⓑ Ⓒ Ⓓ

2. On weekends in Iwate Prefecture, there is a special train that is equipped _____ a planetarium and a gallery.
   (A) with
   (B) by
   (C) on
   (D) for
   Ⓐ Ⓑ Ⓒ Ⓓ

3. A certain mountain village that has become depopulated in recent years may set _____ a council in which citizens can participate directly in the making of municipal decisions.
   (A) in
   (B) up
   (C) down
   (D) aside
   Ⓐ Ⓑ Ⓒ Ⓓ

4. Communities are scattered _____ the mountainous area, where bus services are limited.
   (A) to
   (B) at
   (C) on
   (D) across
   Ⓐ Ⓑ Ⓒ Ⓓ

5. Nearly half of the nation's municipalities could disappear _____ a few decades.
   (A) at
   (B) within
   (C) until
   (D) by
   Ⓐ Ⓑ Ⓒ Ⓓ

Part 6 Text Completion

T-CD 2-13

A word or phrase is missing in some of the sentences below. Four answer choices are given below each of those sentences. Select the best answer to complete the text.

Countryside

Japan's population is decreasing. ___6___ the many consequences of this trend is the fact that the number of local towns is diminishing, too. Small towns and rural areas are the hardest hit. Some localities have simply ceased to exist, and others are being gradually emptied ___7___. At the same time, Japan's population is aging. Aged people now make ___8___ about one-fourth of Japan's population. It is important to preserve Japan's local areas ___9___ developing industries that use regional resources. It is vital that we create an environment where people can raise families and live satisfying lives in their own hometowns.

6. (A) Among　(B) Within
   (C) As　(D) Under
   Ⓐ Ⓑ Ⓒ Ⓓ

7. (A) into　(B) over
   (C) out　(D) up
   Ⓐ Ⓑ Ⓒ Ⓓ

8. (A) over　(B) up
   (C) of　(D) out
   Ⓐ Ⓑ Ⓒ Ⓓ

9. (A) in　(B) off
   (C) of　(D) by
   Ⓐ Ⓑ Ⓒ Ⓓ

Part 7 Reading Comprehension

T-CD 2-14

Choose the best answer for each question.

To: Harriet Sheringham
From: Peter Dickson
Date: May 16
Subject: A problem

Dear Harriet,

Thank you for sending us the office supplies we requested yesterday. They arrived at our department this morning. We sincerely appreciate your quick response and dealing with our order so soon. But there is one problem. The 10 units of the multi-color ink cartridge have arrived, but they don't fit our office's printer. When I checked the product we received, I found that it is an LM 51 series ink cartridge, which is different from the ones that we used before. The cartridge we use is an LM 70 series cartridge. I'm quite sure I asked you on the phone yesterday to send us the LM 70 ones. Could you please check it and arrange for the office supplier to send us the correct ones as soon as possible? — [1] — The rest of the items — the ballpoint pens and the black-and-white ink cartridges — are all the ones I ordered.

Best Regards,

Peter Dickson
Personnel Department

To:	Roger McCloy
From:	Harriet Sheringham
Date:	May 16
Subject:	Mistake

Dear Mr. Roger McCloy,

We ordered some office supplies from you on the 15th of May, and we received them today. — [2] — But one of our staff members emailed me to complain about the multi-color ink cartridges. We found that the ink cartridges you delivered are not the ones we ordered. The cartridge we ordered is an LM 70, not an LM 51. Kindly re-check the order form, and I'm sure you will find that we ordered ten LM 70 cartridges. Could you please send 10 units of the correct cartridges immediately? We need them ASAP — by tomorrow morning at the very latest. — [3] — I would request you to please be careful with our next order. Thank you.

Sincerely,

Harriet Sheringham
Purchasing Department
Beresford Insurance Company

コーヒーブレーク

エミリィ・ディキンスン（Emily Dickinson; 1830-1886）。米文学史上最高の女性詩人

言葉

言葉は話されてしまえば
死んでしまうと
ある人は言う
私は言いたいのだ
まさにその時から
言葉は生き始めるのだ

To: Harriet Sheringham
From: Roger McCloy
Date: May 16
Subject: Re: Mistake

Dear Ms. Harriet Sheringham,

We sincerely apologize to you for sending the wrong items yesterday. After looking into the matter, we found that the fault lies with the staff member who was in charge of packaging and who had accidentally put the wrong cartridges into your package. On receiving your e-mail, we immediately sent five units of the correct multi-color ink cartridges via special delivery, and we're confident that you will receive them by the morning of the 18th. Unfortunately, at the moment, we don't have enough of the ink cartridges in stock to meet your request for ten cartridges. We have sent you the last of our stock. —[4]— We expect a new delivery of this cartridge from the producer to be made in the next few days. As soon as the delivery arrives, we will send you the remaining five cartridges. It goes without saying that there will be no extra delivery charge. We are very sorry to have inconvenienced you. Rest assured that we will not make such a mistake again. We look forward to continuing to serve you in the future.

Sincerely,

Roger McCloy
Customer Service Manager
Dexter Office Supplier

エミリィは言葉がいかに大切かを表現しています。これはアフォリズム(ことわざ的表現)の一種です。言葉は話されてしまえばそれで終わりと言う人もいるけれども、決してそうではなく、むしろその後から言葉が力を持つことがあるというのです。このようにエミリィのアフォリズムには人生の機微をつく表現が多く、このことが人々の心を引きつける要因の一つになりました。

10. What was the complaint about the delivered items?

(A) The wrong type of ink cartridges were delivered.
(B) The delivered cartridges were fewer in number than the number ordered.
(C) The cartridges were the wrong color.
(D) The requested ballpoint pens and black-and-white ink cartridges were not included in the delivery. Ⓐ Ⓑ Ⓒ Ⓓ

11. Which of the following does Harriet most likely NOT expect Roger to do?

(A) To apologize
(B) To resign immediately
(C) To deliver the correct cartridges quickly
(D) Not to make a mistake again Ⓐ Ⓑ Ⓒ Ⓓ

12. What was the cause of the mistake?

(A) The original order requested the wrong item.
(B) Carelessness of a packaging department staff member
(C) A sudden stock shortage
(D) A computer error Ⓐ Ⓑ Ⓒ Ⓓ

13. When will Harriet's office get all of the cartridges they need?

(A) By the evening of May 16th
(B) Tomorrow morning
(C) By the morning of May 18th
(D) Sometime after May 18th Ⓐ Ⓑ Ⓒ Ⓓ

14. In which of the positions marked [1], [2], [3], and [4] does the following sentence best fit?

"We have been doing business with you for a long time, which makes this mistake especially regrettable."

(A) [1]
(B) [2]
(C) [3]
(D) [4] Ⓐ Ⓑ Ⓒ Ⓓ

Unit 15 Mini – TOEIC Test

Part 1 Photographs

30 T-CD 2-15

For each picture, you will hear four short statements. Look at the pictures below and choose the statement that best describes what you see in each picture.

1. 

Ⓐ Ⓑ Ⓒ Ⓓ

2. 

Ⓐ Ⓑ Ⓒ Ⓓ

Part 2 Question-Response

31 T-CD 2-16

Choose the best response to each question or statement you hear.

3. Mark your answer. (A) (B) (C)

4. Mark your answer. (A) (B) (C)

Part 3 Conversations

32 T-CD 2-17

Listen to the conversation. Then choose the best answer to each question below.

Image Crown copyright, UK

5. How long has the woman been driving?
   (A) 2 hours
   (B) 3 hours
   (C) 5 hours
   (D) 7 hours

   (A) (B) (C) (D)

6. What will they do at the service area?
   (A) Use the restroom
   (B) Fill the car with gasoline
   (C) Have a coffee and rest a bit
   (D) Get directions

   (A) (B) (C) (D)

7. What do the speakers plan to do for dinner?
   (A) Eat take-out-food in their car on the way back home
   (B) Eat at the service station
   (C) Wait until they get home
   (D) Skip dinner and go straight to bed

   (A) (B) (C) (D)

Part 4 Talks

33 T-CD 2-18

You will listen to a short talk. Choose the best answer to each question below.

8. Who is this message for?
   (A) Travel agents
   (B) The government
   (C) Drivers
   (D) Weather forecasters
   Ⓐ Ⓑ Ⓒ Ⓓ

9. What is the date today?
   (A) Monday, 26 January
   (B) Sunday, 27 January
   (C) Monday, 26 February
   (D) Sunday, 27 February
   Ⓐ Ⓑ Ⓒ Ⓓ

10. What should the people listening to the message do?
   (A) Leave the North of England immediately
   (B) Help to clear snow from the roads
   (C) Cancel all their weekend plans
   (D) Stay at home if possible
   Ⓐ Ⓑ Ⓒ Ⓓ

コーヒーブレーク

エミリィ・ディキンスン

大草原をつくるには

大草原をつくるにはクローバー１本　蜜蜂１匹で十分だ
クローバー１本と蜜蜂１匹
それに空想
蜜蜂がいなくても空想だけで十分だ

エミリィは人間の想像力や空想に対する大変な信頼を表現しています。「クローバー１本と蜜蜂１匹」とは広大な草原もその原初をたどれば一草一虫からはじまるという意味です。「蜜蜂がいなくても空想だけで十分だ」とは、たとえ蜜蜂がいなくても空想さえあれば大きな世界（大草原）を見ることは可能だと言っているのです。エミリィが（後半生、自宅をほとんど出ることもなく）2 階の自室という狭い領域に閉じこもったままで宇宙的広い世界を見ることが出来たのは、この想像力や空想によるものです。彼女はこれらの深さ、高さ、凝縮力、壮大さ等をテコにして詩を書きあげていったのです。詩人の特性を十分に備えていた証と言えましょう。

Part 5 Incomplete Sentences

T-CD 2-19

Choose the best answer to complete each sentence below.

11. If I don't find a good, high-paying job for the summer, I won't be able to pay my college _____ for the fall semester.
    (A) money
    (B) tuition
    (C) allowance
    (D) salary
    Ⓐ Ⓑ Ⓒ Ⓓ

12. The moment he first met Yoko, he was _____ by her charming smile.
    (A) captivated
    (B) exciting
    (C) surprising
    (D) discouraged
    Ⓐ Ⓑ Ⓒ Ⓓ

13. _____ of soccer, how did your favorite player do in his last game?
    (A) Spoken
    (B) Spoke
    (C) Speaking
    (D) Speak
    Ⓐ Ⓑ Ⓒ Ⓓ

14. Vending machines have become a daily _____ for people on the go.
    (A) necessary
    (B) necessaries
    (C) necessarily
    (D) necessity
    Ⓐ Ⓑ Ⓒ Ⓓ

15. These days coffee is gaining in popularity, as it is viewed as a more _____ drink.
    (A) sophisticated
    (B) sophistication
    (C) sophisticate
    (D) sophisticating
    Ⓐ Ⓑ Ⓒ Ⓓ

Part 6 Text Completion

T-CD 2-20

A word or phrase is missing in some of the sentences below. Four answer choices are given below each of those sentences. Select the best answer to complete the text.

Do you have a Daily Grind Coffee Shop stamp card? For _____ dollar

16. (A) an
(B) each
(C) one
(D) a

you spend (promotional items _____), you get one stamp. When your

17. (A) you excluded
(B) to exclude
(C) excluding
(D) excluded

point card is full, you will receive a free large coffee or bakery item. If you have any questions or require any _____ information, please contact us at

18. (A) further
(B) farther
(C) added
(D) longer

bakeryxx@royal.co.jp

16.	Ⓐ	Ⓑ	Ⓒ	Ⓓ
17.	Ⓐ	Ⓑ	Ⓒ	Ⓓ
18.	Ⓐ	Ⓑ	Ⓒ	Ⓓ

Part 7 Reading Comprehension

T-CD 2-21

Choose the best answer for each question.

Dislike House Cleaning?

Apex Cleaning provides dependable, top-quality cleaning services throughout the Newtown area. We've been in the business for over 25 years, so you know that our company and crew are professional, friendly, and 100% trustworthy. We take special care of every home and clean it just as we would our own. We provide cleaning for every room in the house, including bathrooms, bedrooms, and kitchen. And we also offer a range of special house-cleaning services. Call us today for a free estimate. We will tailor our cleaning services to meet all your household needs. Call us today at (222) 4321 or online at apexcleaning.com.

19. Who most likely will call this company?
   (A) Local businesses
   (B) Home owners or renters
   (C) Home builders
   (D) Home decorators
   Ⓐ Ⓑ Ⓒ Ⓓ

20. What can definitely be said about Apex Cleaning?
   (A) They can finish their job in 24 hours.
   (B) They promise to treat each customer's home like their own.
   (C) They are nationally recognized for their superior work.
   (D) They charge slightly more for bigger jobs.
   Ⓐ Ⓑ Ⓒ Ⓓ

21. Which of the following is NOT true about Apex Cleaning?
   (A) They can design a cleaning schedule to suit each customer's needs.
   (B) They are a new company, but growing rapidly.
   (C) They can be contacted by phone or on their website.
   (D) They do not charge for cleaning estimates.
   Ⓐ Ⓑ Ⓒ Ⓓ